CASINO CRAPS
FOR THE
WINNER

**A STEP-BY-STEP MANUAL
FOR SERIOUS CRAPS PLAYERS**

CASINO CRAPS
CRAPS
FOR THE
WINNER

A STEP-BY-STEP MANUAL
FOR SERIOUS CRAPS PLAYERS

AVERY CARDOZA

CARDOZA PUBLISHING

Cardoza Publishing is the foremost gaming and gambling publisher in the world with a library of more than 200 up-to-date and easy-to-read books and strategies. These authoritative works are written by the top experts in their fields and with more than 10,000,000 books in print, represent the best-selling and most popular gaming books anywhere.

2010 New Edition!

New Edition Copyright © 1982, 1987, 1992, 1998, 2002, 2010 by Avery Cardoza

Library of Congress Catalog Number: 2010921134
ISBN 10:   1-58042-241-1
ISBN 13: 978-1-58042-241-3

Visit our website or write for a full list of Cardoza Publishing books and advanced strategies.

CARDOZA PUBLISHING
P.O. Box 98115, Las Vegas, NV 89193
Toll-Free Phone (800)577-WINS
email: cardozabooks@aol.com
www.cardozabooks.com

CONTENTS

CONTENTS

CONTENTS

TABLES

INTRODUCTION TO THE REVISED EDITION

This updated edition gives you three new chapters and fifteen new charts—plus a bonus chart—including information which have never before appeared in print. You'll get the exact percentages on the main odds games up to two decimal places, and the approximate percentages from single odds (1x) games up to 100x games—plus a win/loss/non-event percentage expectation for every possible combination of points from one point up to all six points being established. Charts also show you how often you can expect to win or lose on the come-out roll, how often a point will be established, and the odds/payoffs/win charts for single odds, full double odds, 3x-4x-5x, 10x and 100x games.

One new chapter takes on questions from ten readers of past editions, addressing their queries and, hopefully, addressing yours as well. The focus of these answers—as well as the focus of this book—is on showing you how to get the best odds possible and beat the casino at craps.

The next time you roll the bones, roll them with the confidence of an informed and confident player, ready to take a big roll to the bank—yours!

# 1. INTRODUCTION

Craps is the most exciting of the casino games, one perfectly tuned to the temperament of action players, for it offers great opportunities to win large sums of money quickly. But big money can be lost just as fast unless you're conversant with the best bets available and know how to use them in a coordinated strategy.

You'll learn everything you need to know about craps—from the rules of the game, how to bet and how to play, to the combinations of the dice and the casino vocabulary. You'll learn the best percentage bets to make and how to use them in winning strategies, and how to bankroll and handle your cash so that you'll manage your money like a pro.

I present winning strategies for players betting with the dice, and for players against the dice, and show the best ways conservative and aggressive players alike can bet their money so that losing streaks are kept to the bare minimum and winning streaks can be taken all the way to the bank!

My winning strategies are based on the soundest principles. By making use of only the best bets available to you, we'll reduce the house edge to the barest minimum. In fact, the bulk of our money will be bet on the free-odds bets, wagers the house has no edge on whatsoever!

All these winning strategies contain built-in betting and money management techniques to make otherwise average wins into big wins, and to restrict losing sessions to affordable amounts. Not only will you learn to win, but you'll be shown how to protect your wins, so that when you leave the table, your wins will be in your pocket and not in your memory. In short, you'll be armed with the most powerful craps strategies available.

Whether you're a high roller betting $100 or $1,000 a throw or just a casual gambler betting $1 chips, you'll find *Casino Craps for the Winner* an indispensable guide to winning, and the only craps book you'll ever need to consult!

So let's get on with it, and let the dice roll!

2. BEGINNER'S GUIDE TO CASINO CRAPS

THE TABLE

The standard casino craps table is rectangular in shape and depending upon the particular size of the casino's table, is built to accommodate between 15 to 24 players. The sides of the table are several feet above the layout where the bets are made, giving the players an edge to lean on, and giving the dice walls to carom off.

THE LAYOUT

The craps layout is divided into three distinct sections. The two end sections, which are identical, are areas around which the players cluster, and where the majority of bets are made. Each end area is run by one of the standing dealers.

The middle area is flanked on either side by a boxman and stickman. This area contains the proposition, or center bets, and is completely under the jurisdiction of the stickman.

The layout is a large piece of green felt with various imprints marking the plethora of bets possible. All action is centered on the layout. Bets are placed, paid off and collected on this felt surface. And, of course, it is on the layout where the dice are thrown.

Layouts around the world are basically the same, though some clubs may have slight variations, but none of these need concern us, for the game of craps is basically the same whatever casino you play in. The minor variations that do occur, concern bets whose odds are so poor that we wouldn't want to make them anyway.

THE DICE

The game of craps is played with two standard six sided dice, with each die numbered from 1 to 6. The dice are manufactured so that they fall as randomly as possible, with a 5 being just as likely to fall on one die as a 3. However, we'll see later that combining two dice together creates some combinations that are more likely to appear than others, and this is the basis of the odds in craps.

PLAYERS

Only one player is needed to play craps, while as many as can fit around a craps table are the maximum. Since there are no seats at craps tables, players will be lined shoulder to shoulder at busy tables. However, when players are winning and numbers are rolling, the crowded quarters only add to the excitement of the table, as opposed to detracting from the fun, unlike calmer games such as blackjack, where players are seated and rarely is more than a few whoops heard from a big win. But at craps, when the action is hot and heavy, bettors will be lined up shoulder to shoulder, screaming, yelling and cajoling for the dice to come through and make them winners.

The following page shows an illustration of a standard Las Vegas craps layout.

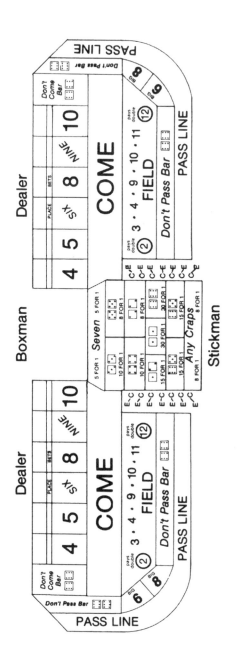

CASINO PERSONNEL

The typical craps table is manned by a crew of four casino employees—one stickman, who stands at the center of the table, two dealers, who stand on the opposite side of the stickman at either end of the table, and a boxman who is seated between the two standing dealers and directly across from the stickman.

Let's look at the function of each crewman in turn.

The Stickman

The **stickman's** main responsibility is the handling of the dice, a task he performs with a flexible, hooked stick. When a new shooter is coming-out, the stickman will offer him a cache of dice to choose from, and after two have been selected, will return the remaining dice to his box.

After each roll of the dice, the stickman will announce the number thrown and bring the dice back to the center of the table. Usually, he will supply additional information about its consequences.

If a 7 is thrown on the come-out roll, he may announce, "7, winner on the pass line."

If instead, a 2, 3 or 12 is rolled on the come-out, he may say, "Craps, line away." When a shooter sevens-out, the stickman might exclaim, "7 out, line away."

A good stickman is a show in himself, and by the excitement he generates, makes the game more lively and colorful for both the players and the dealers. And from the casino's standpoint, happy players tend to bet heavier and wilder than they normally would.

The dice will be returned to the shooter after the dealers have finished making payoffs.

The stickman is also responsible for the proposition, or center bets made in the middle of the layout. He will place all proposition bets directed his way into their proper location on the layout.

If these bets are winners, the stickman will direct the dealers to pay off the winning players, and if the bets are losers, he will collect the lost bets and push them over to the boxman.

The Dealers

There is a dealer located on either side of the boxman, and his main responsibility is to handle all the monetary transactions and betting on his end of the table. He pays off winning bets and collects losing ones, converts cash into chips, and will change chips into higher or lower denominations for the player.

Though you can make many of the bets yourself, there are wagers such as the place bets, certain free-odds bets, and proposition wagers which must be given to the dealer for their placement.

Each standing dealer has a **marker buck**, a plastic disk used to indicate the established point. If a player is coming-out, beginning his roll, the marker buck will be lying on its black side, labeled "**off**," and if a point is established, the dealer will flip the marker buck to the white side, marked "**on**," and place it in the appropriately numbered box to indicate the point.

It is with the dealers that the player will have most of his contact and to whom he can address his questions.

The Boxman

The **boxman** sits between the two dealers and across from the stickman, and from this central position, supervises the running of the craps table. His job is not only to watch over the casinos bankroll, most of which sits right in front of him in huge stacks, but to make sure the dealers make the correct payoffs so that neither the player nor the house gets shorted.

He is responsible for settling any disputes that may arise between the players and the dealers. Generally, the benefit of the doubt will be given to the player on any disputed call. If the dice leave the table for any reason, the returned dice are brought directly to the boxman for inspection. He will check the logo and coded numbers on the dice to make sure they haven't been switched, and will inspect the surfaces for imperfections that may influence the game. If, for any reason, the boxman feels suspicious of the returned dice, he will remove them from play and have the stickman offer the shooter a new pair.

When one boxman is on duty, he will supervise one end of the table while the stickman watches the other.

However, when the action is fast, and stacks of chips are riding on each roll of the dice, a second boxman will often be added to the crew to help watch the table. In these cases, the boxmen will sit next to each other behind the chips, each being responsible for one end of the table.

In addition to the boxmen, there are other supervisors, called floormen and pit bosses, who watch over the action from behind the boxman in the area known as the pit.

The Pit

Craps tables are arranged in a pattern so that a central area, known as the **pit**, is formed in the middle. The tables are arranged around the pit so that the boxmen and standing dealers have their backs to the pit area, and so that the floormen, standing inside the pit, can easily watch over all of the craps tables.

The Floormen

The **floormen** spend their entire shift on their feet, and are responsible for supervising a particular table or group of tables in the pit.

In addition to these supervisory capacities, they deal with players that have established credit lines. If a player requests credit, the floorman checks to see if his credit is good, and if verified, authorizes the dealer to give the requested chips. At the same time, or soon afterwards, he will bring the player an IOU to sign, acknowledging the credit transaction.

The Pit Boss

The **pit boss**, under whose authority the floormen work, is in the charge of the entire craps pit. He's rarely in contact with the players, unless a high roller is playing, whereby he may come over and introduce himself or offer the roller some comps (freebies).

ENTERING A GAME

To enter a craps game, slip into a space by the rail of the craps table. After catching the dealer's attention, place your cash on the layout and inform him of the denomination of chips you would like. The dealer will take your money, and give it to the boxman who will supervise the exchange.

CONVERTING TRAVELLER'S CHECKS AND MONEY ORDERS TO CASH

The dealers will accept only cash or chips at the table, so if you bring traveller's checks, money orders or the like, you must go to the area of the casino marked **Casino Cashier** to get these converted to cash. Be sure to bring proper identification to insure a smooth transaction.

CASINO CHIPS

Chip denominations run in $1, $5, $25, $100, and $500 units. $1 chips are generally referred to as **silver**, $5 chips as **nickels**, $25 chips as **quarters**, and $100 chips as **dollars**. Unless playing at a 25¢ minimum craps table, dollar units are the minimum currency available.

BETTING

Casinos prefer that the player uses chips for betting purposes, for the handling of money at the table is cumbersome and slows the game. However, cash can be used to bet with, though all payoffs will be in chips.

HOUSE LIMITS

The house limits will be posted on placards located on each corner of the table. They will indicate the minimum bet required to play and also the maximum bet allowed.

Minimum bets range from $1 and $5 per bet, to a maximum of $500, $1000 or $2,000 a bet. Occasionally, 25¢ minimum craps tables may be found as well. If special arrangements are made, a player can bet as much as he can muster in certain casinos. The old Horseshoe Casino in Las Vegas, back when Benny Binion ran it, was known to book any bet no matter the size.

In 1981, a man walked into the Horseshoe and placed a bet for $777,777. He bet the don't pass, and walked out two rolls later with one and a half million dollars in cash!

CONVERTING CHIPS INTO CASH

Dealers do not convert your chips into cash. Once you've bought your chips at the table, that cash is dropped into a dropbox, and thereafter unobtainable at the table. When you are ready to convert your chips, take them to the cashier's cage where they'll be changed into cash.

FREE DRINKS AND CIGARETTES

Casinos offer their customers unlimited free drinking while gambling at the tables. In addition to alcoholic beverages, a player can order milk, soft drinks, juices or any other beverages. This is ordered through and served by a cocktail waitress.

Cigarettes and cigars are also complimentary and can be ordered through the cocktail waitress.

TIPPING

Tipping, or **toking**, as it is called in casino parlance, should be viewed as a gratuitous gesture by the player to the crew of dealers he feels has given him good service. Tipping is totally at the player's discretion, and in no way should be considered an obligation.

If you toke, toke only when you're winning, and only if the crew is friendly and helpful to you. Do not toke dealers that you don't like or ones that try to make you feel guilty about not tipping. Dealers that make playing an unpleasant experience for you deserve nothing.

Tips are shared by the crew working the craps table. Though the usual tip is to make a proposition bet, with the exclamation "one for the boys," a better way to toke the crew would be to make a line bet for them, so they can have a good chance of winning the bet. Dealers prefer this type of tip for they too are aware how poor the proposition bets are. This is also better than just handing over the toke, for if the bet is won, the dealer wins double for the tip—the amount bet for him plus the winnings from that bet.

PLAY OF THE GAME AND THE COME-OUT ROLL

When a new player is to throw the dice, the stickman will empty his box of dice and push them across the layout with his stick. After this player, known as the **shooter**, selects two dice of his choice, the stickman will retrieve the remaining dice and return them to his box. In a new game, the player closest to the boxman's left side will receive the dice first, and the rotation of the dice will go clockwise from player to player around the craps table.

The shooter has no advantage over the other players except perhaps the psychological edge he may get throwing the dice himself. He is, however, required to make either a pass or don't pass bet as the shooter. He can also make any other bets allowed.

There are a wide variety of bets the players can make, and these must be placed before the dice are thrown. Players at the table can bet with the dice or against them, at their preference, but in either case, the casino will book all wagers.

Play starts when one of the players, known as the **shooter**, chooses two dice from the dozen or so offered to him by the stickman, shakes them up and rolls them the length of the table.

The shooter is supposed to throw the dice so that they bounce off the far wall of the table. If the throw does not reach the far wall, the shooter will be requested to toss harder on his next throw, and if he persists in underthrowing the dice, the boxman may disallow him from throwing further. This policy protects against cheats that can manipulate unobstructed throws of the dice.

This first roll by the shooter, called the **come-out roll**, will determine immediate winners or losers if it is a 2, 3, 7, 11, or 12, or it will establish a **point**, that is, any of the other throws possible—4, 5, 6, 8, 9, or 10. Here's how it works.

Players making **pass line** wagers, betting that the shooter will "pass," or win, are hoping that the come-out roll is a 7 or an 11, an automatic winner for them. If the roll instead is a 2, 3 or 12, the shooter is said to have **crapped-out**, and that's an automatic loser for pass line bettors. These wagers are made by placing bets in the area marked *Pass Line*.

Players making **don't pass** wagers, betting against the dice, are hoping for just the opposite. A 7 or 11 thrown on the come-out roll is an automatic loser for them, while the 2 and 3 are automatic winners. The 12, if rolled, is a tie for don't pass bettors (In some casinos it's the 2 instead that's a tie and the 12 is a winner.) These wagers are made by placing bets in the area marked *Don't Pass*.

Any other number thrown on the come-out roll, the 4, 5, 6, 8, 9, and 10, becomes the **point**, and the dealers will indicate this by flipping their respective marker bucks to the white side marked "on," and move the disk into the rectangular numbered boxes corresponding to the point number thrown.

Once a point is established, there are only two numbers that matter to pass or don't pass bettors—the 7 and the point. If the 7 is thrown before the point repeats, pass line bettors lose and don't pass bettors win. And if the point repeats before the 7, then the opposite is true; the pass line bettors win, and the don't pass bettors lose. All other throws are immaterial. For example, if the point is a 6, rolls of 12, 3, 8, and 10 are inconsequential. It's only the 7 or the point, the 6 in this example, that affects these wagers.

The **shoot**, as this progression of rolls is called, will continue until the point repeats, a winner for pass line bettors, or until a 7 is rolled, called **sevening-out**, a loser on the pass line but a winner for don't pass bettors. In either case, a point repeating or a seven out, the following roll will be a new come out roll, the beginning of a new progression.

The shooter can continue to roll the dice until he either sevens out or voluntarily gives up the dice. And then, in a clockwise direction, each successive player gets a chance to be the shooter (though a player may decline and pass the privilege to the next player). Even though the shooter may **crap-out** (the throw of a 2, 3 or 12) on his come-out roll, a losing roll for pass line bettors, the shooter does not have to yield the dice. It is only when he throws a 7 before his point repeats, *sevens-out*, that the dice must be relinquished.

There is no benefit to being a shooter other than the pleasure you get shaking, rattling and rolling the dice to the screams and encouragement of your fellow players—and, as craps players feel, "controlling" your own destiny. The only requirement you have as a shooter, other than throwing the dice, is to make either a pass or don't pass bet.

Winning pass and don't pass bets pay even-money, for every dollar wagered, a dollar is won.

There are many other bets available to you as we will discuss later, some that can be made only after a point is established, and others that can be made at any time during a shoot. So while the line bettors may not be affected by a particular throw, the dealers may be paying off or collecting chips on other affected wagers while the shoot is in progress.

THE COME-OUT ROLL CAPSULATED

The come-out roll occurs when:
1. A new shooter takes the dice.
2. The shooter throws a 2, 3, 7, 11, or 12 on the come-out roll, an automatic winner or loser for the line bettors.
3. After a point is established, the shooter either re-peats that point or sevens-out.

BETTING RIGHT OR WRONG

Betting right or wrong are only casino terms used to designate whether a player is betting with the dice, **betting right**, or betting against the dice, **betting wrong**, and are in no way indicative of a correct or incorrect way of playing. As we shall see, both ways of betting are equally valid.

 # 3. UNDERSTANDING THE ODDS

Knowing how to figure the possible combinations that can occur when two dice are thrown is essential to understanding the basics of craps—the bets, the odds and the payoffs. You'll be surprised at how simple the odds really are, and will find craps to be a more rewarding experience once you learn these fundamentals.

Craps is played with two dice, individually called die, and each die is a near perfect six sided cube, guaranteed to be within 1/10,000 of an inch accurate.

Each die has six equally possible outcomes when thrown— numbers one through six. The two dice thrown together have a total of 36 possible outcomes, the six combinations of one die by the six combinations of the other. The chart below shows these combinations. Notice how certain totals have more possibilities of being thrown, or are more probable of occurring, by the random throw of the two dice.

COMBINATIONS OF THE DICE

NUMBER THROWN	COMBINATIONS	NUMBER OF COMBINATIONS
2		1
3		2
4		3
5		4
6		5
7		6
8		5
9		4
10		3
11		2
12		1

You can see by the illustration that the 7 is more likely to be thrown than any other number, having six possible combinations. Next in frequency are the 6 and the 8, five outcomes each, then the 5 and the 9, four outcomes, the 4 and the 10, three outcomes apiece, the 3 and the 11, two outcomes, and finally, the 2 and the 12, one combination each.

A SHORTCUT TO REMEMBERING THE ODDS

Notice the symmetry of combinations on either side of the 7. The 6 and 8 have equal possibilities of being thrown, just as the 5 and 9, 4 and 10, 3 and 11, and 2 and 12 do.

If you take rolls of 7 and below and subtract one from that number, you arrive at the correct number of combinations for that roll. Thus, there are four ways to roll a 5 (5-1), six ways to roll a 7 (7-1) and one way to roll a 2 (2-1).

For numbers greater than the 7, match that number with the corresponding symmetrical number on the other side of the 7, and subtract one. Thus, to find the combinations of the 8, you match it with the 6 (which has an equal likelihood of occurring), and subtracting one, you get five combinations.

FIGURING THE ODDS OF ROLLING A SPECIFIC NUMBER

To figure the odds of rolling any particular number, divide the number of combinations for that particular number into 36, the total number of combinations possible.

Let's say the 7. There are six ways to roll a 7. Dividing the six combinations into 36, the total number of combinations, we find the odds of rolling a 7 on any one roll is one in six (6/36 reduced to 1/6), or equivalently, 5 to 1. The chart below shows the odds of rolling a number on any one roll.

ODDS OF ROLLING THE NUMBERS

	Combinations	Chance of Being Rolled	Expressed in Odds
2 or 12	1	1/36	35 to 1
3 or 11	2	2/36	17 to 1
4 or 10	3	3/36	11 to 1
5 or 9	4	4/36	8 to 1
6 or 8	5	5/36	6.2 to 1
7	6	6/36	5 to 1

The listing of two numbers together such as the 5 or 9 is done to abbreviate. The odds apply to either the 5 or the 9, not to both together.

UNDERSTANDING THE TERMINOLOGY

Correct Odds, House Payoff & Edge

The **house advantage** or **edge** is the difference between the player's chances of winning the bet, called the **correct odds**, and the casino's actual payoff, called the **house payoff** or simply, the **payoff**. For example, the correct odds of rolling a 7 are 5 to 1. Since the house will pay only 4 to 1 should the 7 be thrown, they maintain an edge of 16.67% on this wager.

To play craps intelligently and better understand the choices available to him, the player must first and foremost be aware of the house advantage on every bet he will ever make, for that, in the long run, determines the player's chances of winning.

Five for One, Five to One

Sometimes on a layout you will see payoffs represented as *for* instead of the usual *to*, such as 9 for 1. This means that the payoff will be a total of nine units, eight winning chips along with your original bet, a house subterfuge to increase its edge over the player. The usual 9 to 1 payoff means nine winning chips and your original bet returned, for a total of 10 units.

Beware of any payoffs with the *for*. As a rule, this type of bet has poor odds to begin with and we wouldn't want to make it anyway, with the *to* or the *for*.

4. THE BETS

Craps offers you a wide variety of possible wagers, with each bet having its own characteristics and inherent odds. Some bets, which we will refer to as **sequence bets**, may require a series of rolls before the outcome is determined, while the outcome of others, called **one-roll bets**, is determined on the very next roll.

Some bets are paid off by the house at **even-money**, for every dollar wagered, the player wins a dollar, while other bets have payoffs as high as 30 to 1. However, as you will see, generally the higher the house payoff, the worse the odds are for the player.

And the odds of the bet, that is, the mathematical house return on every dollar wagered, is your most important concern. To have the best chances of winning, you must avoid all the sucker bets, and make only the best bets available.

A. MOST ADVANTAGEOUS BETS

The bets presented in this section have the lowest built-in house edge of all the bets in craps, and one bet, the free-odds bet, gives the house no advantage whatsoever. These bets, the pass, don't pass, come, don't come, and the free-odds bets, are the most important bets a player can make, and are the foundation of our winning strategies.

THE LINE BETS— PASS AND DON'T PASS

These even-money bets can only be made on a come-out roll, before a point is established, and give the house an edge of only 1.4%. And when backed by the free-odds wagers, the overall house edge drops to 0.8% in a single odds game and to 0.6% in a double odds game.

Pass Line

Players making pass line bets are wagering that the dice will **pass**, or win, and are called *right bettors*. Pass line bets are also referred to as **front line bets**, and are made by placing the wager in the area marked pass line.

On the come-out roll, a throw of a 7 or 11 is an automatic winner for the pass line bettors while the throw of a craps, a 2, 3, or 12, is an automatic loser. If any other number is thrown, the 4, 5, 6, 8, 9, or 10, then that number is established as the point, and the shooter must repeat the point before a 7 is thrown for pass line bettors to win. The throw of a 7 before the point repeats is a loser for pass line bettors, called sevening-out, and the dealers will collect the lost bets.

Once the point is established, only the 7 and the point number affect the pass line bettor. All other numbers have no bearing on the bet and can be considered neutral throws.

Let's look at three progressions to see how the pass line bet works.

1. The come-out roll is a 5, establishing 5 as the point. The following roll is a 2, a neutral throw, for a point has already been established. An 8 is then thrown, still having no bearing on the outcome, and then a 5. The point was repeated, or *made*, before the seven was thrown, and the pass line bettors win their bets.

2. The come-out roll is a 7, an automatic winner for the pass line bettors, and they are paid off by the dealers. Since the progression has been completed, the following roll will be another come-out roll.

3. Here is a losing proposition. The come-out roll is a 9, establishing 9 as the point. The shooter then rolls a 6, then a 12, and then an 11. All three rolls are neutral since a point is already established. The following roll is a 7. Since the 7 was rolled before the 9, the shooter's point repeated, pass line bettors lose and the dealer will collect their bets. A new come-out roll will ensue.

PASS LINE CAPSULATED

Payoff:	Even-Money
House Edge:	1.4%
Automatic Winners:	7 or 11 on the come-out roll.
Automatic Losers:	2, 3, or 12 on the come-out roll.

If a point is established on the come-out roll,
the pass line bettor:
Wins by the point repeating before the 7 is thrown.
Loses by the roll of a 7 before the point repeats.

Don't Pass

Players betting don't pass are called *wrong bettors*, and are betting against the dice. Don't pass bets are also called **back line bets** and are made by placing the wager in the area marked don't pass.

On the come-out roll, a throw of a 2 or 3 is an automatic winner for the don't pass bettors, while a 7 or an 11 is an automatic loser. The 12 is a standoff between the back line bettor and the house. (In some casinos the 2 is the standoff and the 12 is the automatic winner. Either way it makes no difference, for there is only one way to throw the 2 or 12.)

Once the point is established, don't pass bettors win by having the 7 thrown before the shooter repeats his point, and lose by the point being repeated before the shooter sevens-out. Here are some progressions to illustrate the don't pass wager.

1. The come-out roll is a 6, establishing 6 as the point. The following rolls are a 5 (no bearing on the outcome), then a 12 (still no bearing) and then a 7. Since the 7 was rolled before the 6 repeated, don't pass bettors win.

2. The come-out roll is a 3, an automatic winner for the don't pass bettor.

3. The come-out roll is a 4, establishing 4 as the point. A 3 is then rolled (neutral), and then a 4, a loss for the back line bettors since the point repeated before the 7 was rolled.

DON'T PASS LINE CAPSULATED

Payoff:	Even-Money
House Edge:	1.4%
Automatic Winners:	2 (or 12) and 3 on the come-out roll.
Automatic Losers:	7 or 11 on the come-out roll.
Standoff:	12 (or 2 in some casinos) on the come-out roll.

If a point is established on the come-out roll,
don't pass bettors:
Win by the throw of a 7 before the point repeats.
Lose by the point repeating before the 7 throws.

COME AND DON'T COME BETS

The come and don't come bets work according to the same rules as the pass and don't pass bets except that these bets can only be made *after* a point is established. The pass and don't pass wagers, on the other hand, can only be made on a come-out roll, *before* a point is established.

The advantage of these bets are that they allow you to cover more points as a right or wrong bettor at the same low 1.4% house edge. And like the line bets, the overall house edge drops to 0.8% when backed by single odds, and 0.6% when backed by double odds.

Come bets are made by putting the chips into the area marked come, while don't come bets are placed in the don't come box. Won bets are paid at even-money

Come Bets

We follow the play of the come bets just as we would with the pass line bets. A 7 or 11 on the first throw following the placing of the bet is an automatic winner, while a 2, 3 or 12 is an automatic loser.

Any other number thrown, the 4, 5, 6, 8, 9, or 10, establishes the point for that come bet, called the **come point**, and the dealer will move the bet from the come box into the large rectangular numbered boxes located at the top of the layout to mark the come point.

Once the come point is established, the bet is won if the come point repeats before the shooter sevens-out, and lost if the 7 is rolled before the point repeats. All other throws are inconsequential on this bet. Won bets will be paid off and removed from the layout.

You can make continuous come bets until all the points are covered if you desire. Thus, it is possible, for the throw of a 7 to simultaneously wipe out several established come bets. On the other hand, a hot shooter rolling point numbers can bring frequent winners to aggressive come bettors.

Let's follow a progression where the right bettor makes both pass line and come bets.

Player Bets: $5 on the pass line.
The come-out roll is a 5, establishing 5 as the point.

Player Bets: $5 on the come.
The roll is an 8, establishing 8 as the come point. The dealer moves the $5 come bet to the rectangular box marked 8 to indicate that 8 is the point for that come bet. In effect, the player has two points working, the 5 and the 8, and decides to make another come bet.

Player Bets: $5 on the come.
The roll is a 6. The dealer moves this new come bet to the 6, the come point for this bet. The other two points are not affected by this roll.

Player Bets: The player has three points established, the 5, 6, and 8, and makes no more bets at this time.
The roll is a 5, a $5 winner on the pass line. It is paid off and removed from the layout, leaving the player with two come points, the 6 and 8.

Player Bets: $5 on the pass line. Since the next roll is a come-out roll and the player wants to cover another point, he bets the pass.
The roll is a 10, establishing 10 as the point.

Player Bets: No additional bets at this time.
The roll is a 2 (neutral on all established bets), then an 8 is thrown, a $5 winner on the come point of 8, and that bet is paid off and removed. The following roll is not a come-out roll, for the come point was made, not the pass line point, the 10.

Player Bets: Wishing to establish a third point, $5 is bet on the come.

The roll is a 7. While the 7 is a $5 winner for the new come bet, it is a loser for the two established points, and they are removed from the layout by the dealer.

The roll of the 7 cleared the layout, and the following roll will be a new come-out roll.

Don't Come Bets

Like the don't pass wager, a 7 or 11 on the first roll following a don't come bet is an automatic loser and the 2 and 3 are automatic winners, 12 being a standoff. (In casinos where the 2 is a standoff and the 12 a winner on the don't pass, the same will hold true for the don't come bets.)

If a 4, 5, 6, 8, 9, or 10 is thrown, establishing a point for the don't come bet, the dealer will move the chips behind the appropriate point box to mark the don't come point. Don't come bettors now win by having the 7 thrown before that point is made. Other numbers, as with the don't pass bets, are neutral rolls. Only the 7 and the come point determine the bet.

Let's follow a progression where the wrong bettor makes both don't pass and don't come bets.

Player Bets: $5 on the don't pass.

The roll is a 10, establishing 10 as the point.

Player Bets: Continuing to bet against the dice, the player now makes a $5 bet on the don't come.

The roll is a 2, a $5 winner on the new don't come bet, and that bet is paid off and removed.

Player Bets: $5 on the don't come.

The roll is a 6. The dealer moves the bet from the don't come area to the upper section of the box numbered 6 to indicate that 6 is the point for this don't come bet. The player now has two points working, the 10 and 6, and decides to establish a third point.

Player Bets: $5 on the don't come.

The roll is a 10, a $5 loser on the don't pass since the point repeated before a 7 was thrown. The don't come point of 6 is unaffected, and the new don't come bet is moved to the 10 box, since 10 is the come point for the new don't come wager.

Player Bets: The player decides not to make any more bets, being content with his bets on points 6 and 10, unwilling to place more bets on the layout. If he were to make another bet against the dice, he would bet don't pass for the next throw is a come-out roll.

The roll is 7, winner on both established come points, and they are paid off and removed. The next roll will be a new come-out roll.

FREE-ODDS BETS

Though not indicated anywhere on the layout, the free-odds bets are the best bets you can make at craps; in fact, they are an indispensable part of your winning strategies. The free-odds bets are so named, for, unlike the other bets at craps, the house has no advantage over the player. Hence, the term free-odds.

However, to make a free-odds bet, you must first have placed a pass, don't pass, come, or don't come wager. When backed by single odds, the overall odds of the pass, don't pass, come, and don't come bets drop to 0.8%, and where double odds are allowed and utilized, the overall odds drop to only 0.6% against you. These are the best odds you can get at single or double odds craps. (Slightly better odds can be achieved in games offering players greater multiple odds bets.)

Free-Odds—Pass Line

Once a point is established on the come-out roll, pass line bettors are allowed to make an additional bet, called a **free-odds bet**, that their point will be repeated before a 7 is thrown. This bet is paid off at the correct odds, giving the house no edge, and is made by placing the chips behind the pass line wager and just outside the pass line area.

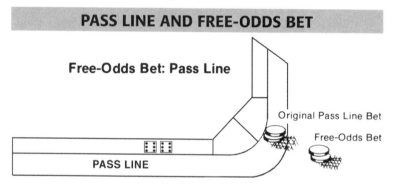

PASS LINE AND FREE-ODDS BET

Free-Odds Bet: Pass Line

Original Pass Line Bet

Free-Odds Bet

PASS LINE

When single odds are allowed, you can bet up to the amount wagered on your pass line bet, and in certain instances, which we'll cover, you can bet more. When double odds are allowed, you can bet twice your pass line bet as a free-odds wager.

Though you can bet less than the permissible amount on the free-odds wager and are allowed to reduce or remove this bet at any time, you should never do so, for the free-odds wagers are the most advantageous bets in craps, and should be fully taken advantage of.

Following is a table which shows the correct odds of the point repeating before a 7 is thrown and the house payoff. Note how the house takes no percentage advantage on these bets since the payoff is identical to the correct odds.

ODDS OF POINT REPEATING BEFORE A SEVEN		
Point Number	**Correct Odds**	**House Payoff**
4 or 10	2 to 1	2 to 1
5 or 9	3 to 2	3 to 2
6 or 8	6 to 5	6 to 5

The odds presented in this table are easy to figure for the only numbers that affect the free-odds bet are the point number, which is a winner, and the 7, which is a loser. All other throws are inconsequential.

There are three ways to roll a winning 4 or 10, and six ways to roll a losing 7, thus 2 to 1 is the correct odds on points 4 or 10. A 5 or 9 can be rolled four ways each against the same six ways of rolling a 7, thus the correct odds are 3 to 2 against the 5 or 9. A 6 or 8 can be made by five combinations, and again, since there are six ways to roll a losing 7, the correct odds are 6 to 5 against the 6 or 8.

Special Allowances—
Single Odds Game

To make the payoffs easier, most casinos will allow you to make a single odds bet greater than your pass line (or come) bet in the following instances.

1. With a pass line bet such as $5 or $25 and the point being a 5 or 9, the casino will allow you to make an odds bet of $6 and $30, respectively, behind the line. If the bet is won, the 3 to 2 payoff on the $6 free-odds bet would be $9, and on the $30 bet, $45.

    If you weren't allowed this special allowance, you would be unable to get the full correct odds on the $5 or $25 free-odds bet since the $1 or more minimum craps tables do not deal in half dollars.

2. With a three unit bet such as $3 or $15, and the point being a 6 or 8, the casino will allow a five unit free-odds bet behind the line. This allows you to take full advantage of the 6 to 5 payoff on points 6 and 8. In the above examples, $5 and $25 free-odds bets would be permitted, and if won, would pay you $6 and $30, respectively.

A three unit bet translates to $3 for the $1 bettor, $15 for the $5 bettor, $30 for the $10 bettor, and so on. Any bet that can be divisible by three can be considered a three unit bet and be backed by the special allowance single odds bets.

A $30 bet on the pass line can be backed by only $30 if the point is a 5 or 9 since the 3 to 2 payoff can be made on this amount, but if the point is a 6 or an 8, can be backed by $50 (five unit special allowance).

If uncertain about the amounts you are allowed to wager as a free odds bet for your pass line bet, simply ask the dealer, and he will let you know the permissible amount.

THREE UNIT BET • SINGLE ODDS SPECIAL ALLOWANCE

Basic Three Unit Bet	6 or 8 as Point	
$3	$5	($6)
$15	$25	($30)
$30	$50	($60)
$45	$75	($90)
$75	$125	($150)
$300	$500	($600)

The first column, Basic Three Unit Bet, is what our standard pass and come bet is, while the second column shows the special allowance permitted when the point is 6 or 8. Numbers in parenthesis indicate the amount paid if the single odds bet is won.

Note that this is only a partial listing of the basic three unit bets, and many more are possible for the player that wants to bet in different ranges than shown.

No special allowances are allowed when the 4 or 10 are established as points for they are easily paid off at 2 to 1 no matter the amount wagered.

On bets smaller than $5 with the point being a 6 or 8, single odds bets will not be able to receive the full 6 to 5 payoff, and will be paid off at even-money only, for again, the craps tables do not stock units smaller than $1 chips.

On bets larger than $5 but in unequal multiples of $5, the free-odds bet will be paid to the highest multiple of $5 at 6 to 5, and the remainder will be paid at even-money. Thus, a $12 odds bet on the 8 will yield a payoff of only $14, $12 on the first $10 (at 6 to 5), and even-money on the unequal remainder of $2.

When the free-odds bets do not receive their full payoff, the bet works to your disadvantage. Therefore, it is recommended that pass and come wagers be made in multiples of $3. This allows you to take full advantage of the special allowances and lowers the overall house edge for the single odds game below 0.8%.

Double Odds—Pass Line

Double odds work just like single odds except that you are allowed to bet double your pass line bet as a free-odds wager. If $10 was bet on the pass line and a 5 was established as the point, the double odds game would allow you to bet $20 as a free-odds wager and receive the same correct 3 to 2 odds on that point, instead of only being allowed a $10 free-odds bet as in the single odds game.

When combined with the pass line bet, double odds brings the overall house edge down to only 0.6%, the best odds you can get at craps (except for games offering higher free-odds multiples). Therefore, when there is a choice of playing a single or double odds game, choose the latter. You want to take advantage of every favorable option allowed.

If you're uncertain whether double odds are allowed, just ask the dealer, and he will let you know. That's what he's there for!

Special Allowances— Double Odds Game

There is one special allowance to keep in mind when playing the double odds game. With a two unit bet on the pass line and a 6 or 8 as the point, a double odds game permits you to wager five units as a free-odds bet. Thus, with a $10 bet (two $5 unit chips), and the point a 6 or 8, a $25 double odds bet would be allowed. If you win, the 6 to 5 payoff would bring $30 in winnings (six $5 chips, an easier payoff for the casino).

I recommend that you bet in multiples of two so you can take advantage of the special five unit allowance when the point is a 6 or an 8. Note that any bet which can be divisible by two can be considered a two unit bet and be backed by the special five unit allowance.

TWO UNIT BET · DOUBLE ODDS SPECIAL ALLOWANCE			
Basic 2-Unit Bet*	**6 or 8 as Point**		**4,5,9 or 10 as Point**
$2	$5	($6)	$4
$10	$25	($30)	$20
$20	$50	($60)	$40
$30	$75	($90)	$60
$50	$125	($150)	$100
$200	$500	($600)	$400

*The Basic Two Unit Bet is our standard pass and come bet. The third column is the normal double odds allowance for points 4, 5, 9, and 10.

Numbers in parenthesis indicate the amount paid if the double odds bet is won (at 6 to 5 payoff).

Note that other two unit bets than those shown in the chart are possible.

Let's follow a sample sequence to see how the free-odds bet works in a single odds game.

We start out with a $15 bet on the pass line. The come-out roll is a 6. Taking advantage of the special five unit allowance, $25 is wagered as a free-odds bet behind the line. (This is placed by the player.)

If the shooter throws a 7 before the point repeats, you lose the $15 pass bet and the $25 free-odds bet, but should the point be rolled before the 7, $15 will be won on the pass line bet and $30 on the odds bet ($25 paid at 6 to 5).

If the game was a double odds game, you could have backed the $15 pass bet with a $30 free-odds bet. And if the point was a 6, the free-odds bet would pay $36 if won ($30 at 6 to 5 = $30).

Free-Odds—Don't Pass

Once the point is established, don't pass bettors are allowed to make a free-odds bet that a 7 will be rolled before the point repeats. The bet is paid off at correct odds, the house enjoying no edge, and is made by placing the free-odds bet next to the don't pass wager in the don't pass box.

DON'T PASS AND FREE-ODDS BET

Free-Odds Bet: Don't Pass

free-odds bet

original don't pass bet

Don't Pass Bar

Since the odds favor the don't pass bettor once the point is established, there being more ways to roll a winning 7 than any individual point number, the don't pass bettor must *lay odds,* put more money on the free-odds bet than he will win.

Let's say the point is a 4. The don't pass bettor's chances of winning the bet are now 2 to 1 in his favor. There are only three ways to roll a 4, a loser, against the six combinations of a 7, a winner. Therefore, the don't pass bettor must bet $20 to win $10 when the point is a 4 (or 10).

(On the other side of the bet, pass line bettors are receiving 2 to 1 odds, for their bet is the underdog, having only three winning chances against six losing combinations.)

To lay odds as a don't pass bettor, the allowable free-odds bet is determined by the *payoff,* not the original bet. Using the above example of a $10 bet on the don't pass with 4 established as the point, the don't pass bettor in a single odds game is allowed up to a $10 win on the free-odds bet. Since the odds are 2 to 1 in his favor, the don't pass bettor must lay $20 to win $10. If it was a double odds game, meaning the player could win $20 on his original $10 bet, than at 1 to 2 odds, $40 would have to be staked for a potential win of $20.

The odds the don't pass bettor must lay are exactly opposite the odds pass line bettors take on the same points. Below is a table showing the free-odds bets from the wrong bettors position.

ODDS OF ROLLING A SEVEN BEFORE POINT REPEATS		
Point Number	**Correct Odds**	**House Payoff**
4 or 10	1 to 2	1 to 2
5 or 9	2 to 3	2 to 3
6 or 8	5 to 6	5 to 6

Note how the house has no percentage advantage on these bets since the payoff is identical to the correct odds.

Like the free-odds bets for right bettors, don't pass free-odds wagers can be removed or reduced at any time, but since these are the player's best bets, it should not be done.

Let's look at a quick example to see how the free-odds bet works for the don't pass bettor.

$10 is bet on the don't pass, and the come-out roll is a 9. The wrong bettor bets $15 behind the line as a free-odds bet, the maximum allowed in a single odds game. He stands to win $10 on the free-odds bet if the 7 is rolled before the 9 repeats, in addition to $10 on his don't pass bet.

Should the point be rolled before the 7, the $15 free-odds bet and $10 don't pass bet will be lost. If double odds were allowed, $20 would be the maximum allowable free-odds win. At 2 to 3 odds, the don't pass bettor would have to lay $30 to win $20.

WRONG BETTORS SPECIAL ALLOWANCES

Single Odds Game

The casino makes a special provision for don't pass bettors when the point is a 5 or 9 and an odd figure such as $5 is wagered. Since the craps tables do not deal in half dollars, the player is allowed to make a free-odds bet of $9 behind the line in this instance, and if the bet is won, will get paid $6 ($9 at 2 to 3).

Whenever the point is 5 or 9 and the original bet is unequal, the house will allow the player to bet more than the straight single odds. Just ask the dealer the exact amount allowed in those instances for the rules may vary from casino to casino.

Free-Odds—Come and Don't Come

Once a come point is established, you can take odds (or lay odds for don't come bettors) and get the same advantageous payoffs, 2-1 on points 4 and 10 (1-2 for wrong bettors), 3-2 on the 5 and 9 (2-3), and 6-5 on the 6 and 8 (5-6).

The house has no advantage on these free-odds wagers, and like the line bets, the overall house edge on the come or don't come bets teamed with single odds drops to 0.8%, and with double odds, to 0.6%.

The same special allowances apply for the come bets. In a single odds game; a three unit bet can be backed by five units if the point is 6 or 8, while a free-odds bet on points 5 and 9 can be backed by additional chips if the original come bet is uneven. In the double odds game, a two unit wager can be backed by five units if the point is a 6 or 8.

However, the odds bets on the come and don't come bets are placed differently than line bets. Rather than being made by the player, the odds bets are given to the dealer to place with the instruction, "odds on the come," or "odds on the don't come."

The dealer will place the odds bet in the appropriate box atop the come point, but slightly offset, so that the odds bet can be differentiated from the come bet.

COME, DON'T COME AND FREE-ODDS BETS

Dealer will place free-odds bet atop original bet but offset to distinguish from come or don't come bet.

	don't come and free-odds bet
8 NINE **10** come and free-odds bet	

The only other difference is with the come bet. While the come bet itself is working on the come-out roll, the odds bet on that come bet is not. Let's say you had $15 on the come point of 6 and that bet was backed by a $25 free-odds bet. A come-out roll of a 7 would, of course, be a loser for the $15 come bet as that bet is always working, but since the free-odds bet was off, the $25 single odds wager would be returned to you.

If a 6 was rolled instead, a winner for the come bet, you would only win the $15, and the $25 odds bet would be returned to you.

Though it is standard procedure for the free-odds bet backing the come wager to be off on the come-out roll, you can request the odds bet to be "on" by informing the dealer that the "odds are on for the come bet." In that case, of course, the odds bet is subject to the normal rules and can be won or lost if the point is made or a 7 is thrown.

The odds on the don't come bets, as with the pass and don't pass wagers, are always working.

Let's look at some betting sequences to illustrate how the free-odds bets on come and don't come wagers work in conjunction with the line bets.

Right Bettors —
(Pass and Come Bets)

Player A is a right bettor, he likes betting with the dice. His standard betting unit is $15 (3 units of $5) and this allows him to take advantage of the special free-odds allowances when the points are 5 and 9, and 6 and 8.

SINGLE ODDS GAME

Player Bets: $15 on the pass line.

The come-out roll is an 8, establishing 8 as the point.

Player Bets: $25 odds bet behind the 8 (5 unit special allowance bet). $15 on the come.

The roll is a 4, establishing the 4 as a come point. Dealer moves Player A's bet from the come line to the box marked 4.

Player Bets: $15 odds bet on the 4. The dealer places the wager on the come bet but at a tilt to show it's an odds bet. Player A decides to make another $15 come bet.

The roll is an 11. The new come bet is an automatic winner for $15. The other bets are unaffected.

Player Bets: $15 more on the come.

The roll is a 4, a winner on that come point. Player A wins $15 on the come bet and $30 (2 to 1 payoff) on the free-odds bet. The new $15 come bet is moved to the place box of 4, to indicate that it's a come point.

Player Bets: $15 odds on the come point of 4.
$15 more on the come.
Player A now has a $15 pass line bet backed by $25 odds on the point of 8, a $15 come bet backed by $15 odds on the point of 4, and a new $15 come wager.

The roll is an 8, a winner on the pass line. Player A gets paid $15 on the pass line bet and $30 on his odds bet (6 to 5 odds) and these bets are removed from the layout. The new come bet is moved to the 8 box, the come point for that last bet. A new come-out roll will follow since the point was made.

Player Bets: $15 on the passline.
   $25 odds bet on his come point of 8.

The roll is a 7, a $15 winner on the new passline bet, but a loser for the two come points of 4 and 8. Since the odds bets were off on the come-out roll, the $15 odds on the 4 and $25 odds on the 8 are returned to the player, leaving the player with only a $30 loss on the come points themselves, but a $15 winner on the pass line bet.

Player A won $120 in bets and lost only $30 for a net win of $90.

Wrong Bettors—
(Don't Pass and Don't Come Bets)

Player B is a wrong bettor, he prefers to bet against the dice. His standard betting unit is $20 because it's easier to figure the laying of odds with bets in multiples of $10.

SINGLE ODDS GAME
Player Bets: $20 on the don't pass.
The come-out roll is a 6, establishing the 6 as a point.

Player Bets: $24 free-odds bet behind the 6 (laying 5 to 6 odds).
   $20 on the don't come.

The roll is a 3, craps, a winner on the new don't come bet. The other bets are unaffected. The winning bet is removed from the layout.

Player Bets: $20 on the don't come again.

The roll is a 10, and the dealer moves the don't come bet above the box marked 10 to indicate the come point for the don't come bet.

Player Bets: $40 free-odds on the come point of 10, (laying 1 to 2 odds). The dealer places the odds bet atop the original bet but at a tilt so the bet can be a distinguished from the don't come bet. He also makes a $20 bet in the don't come box.

The roll is a 9, establishing 9 as the come point for the new don't come bet. Player B now has bets against three points, the 6, 9, and 10. The roll of any of those point numbers is a loss for Player B on that particular number rolled, while the throw of a 7 will be a winner on all.

Player Bets: $30 free-odds on the 9, and decides not to make any more don't come bets.

The roll is a 6, a loser on the don't pass. Player B loses that $20 bet and the $24 odds bet behind it. Since the point was made, the next roll is a new come-out roll. All bets for the wrong bettor will be working.

Player Bets: $20 on the don't pass.

The roll is an 8, establishing 8 as the come point on the new don't pass bet.

Player Bets: $24 odds on the come point of 8, and decides not to make any further bets at this time.

The roll is a 7, a simultaneous winner on all the don't pass, don't come, and odds bets. Player B wins $20 per wrong bet plus the $20 odds behind each bet for a $40 win per point. With three points covered, the total win on that 7 was $120.

Player B won $140 in bets and lost only $44 for a net win of $96.

B. THE REST OF THE BETS

With the exception of the place bet of 6 and 8, none of the bets presented in this section, which include the remainder of the bets possible at craps, are recommended for play. The house edge over the player on these bets is too large to be incorporated into a winning strategy, and the player making these bets will soon find himself drained of significant portions of his bankroll.

In fact, the majority of bets listed here are sucker bets, wagers that give the house an edge so exorbitant that the player stands no more than a slim chance of winning. Just because a bet is exotic looking and available doesn't mean that it should be bet on. To do well at craps, all bets with prohibitive odds must be avoided.

The bets listed in this section are discussed anyway so that you have a full understanding of all the bets possible at craps, and so that you are never tempted to make these poor wagers.

PLACE BETS

The **place bets** are among the most popular wagers in craps, and are a bet that a particular point number, whichever is wagered on, the 4, 5, 6, 8, 9, or 10, is rolled before a 7 is thrown. You can make as many place bets as you want, and some players do, covering all the numbers with place bets.

However, this is not recommended strategy, for as we will see, with the exception of the place bets of 6 and 8, the other place bets, the 4, 5, 9, and 10, are poor wagers, and will have no role in our winning strategies.

Place bets are made by giving the dealer the desired wager, and telling him, for example, "to place the 9," or any such statement that indicates you want to make a place bet on the 9.

Though place bets can be made at any time, they are not working, or are "**off**" on the come-out roll, unless you request them to be "**on**" (working).

You can also request your place bets to be off for a limited series of throws, and you may increase, reduce or remove them at any time prior to a roll.

HOUSE PAYOFFS ON PLACE BETS			
Bet	**Payoff**	**Correct Odds**	**House Advantage**
4 or 10	9 to 5	2 to 1	6.67%
5 or 9	7 to 5	3 to 2	4.00%
6 or 8	7 to 6	6 to 5	1.52%

To get the full payoffs on the place bets, you should make your bets in the proper multiples. On place bets of 4 and 10, and 5 and 9, the bets should be made in multiples of $5 since the payoffs are 9 to 5 and 7 to 5 respectively. On the 6 and 8, the bet should be in multiples of $6 (7 to 6 payoff).

Excess bets in unequal multiples will be paid off at even-money only and work to your disadvantage. For example, a $10 bet on the 6 will be paid as follows. The first $6 will get the full 7 to 6 odds for $7, while the remaining $4 gets paid at even-money, or $4, for a total win of $11. The last $4, paid off at only even-money, is a terrible payoff, and makes the entire bet a poor one.

Unless you make the place bets of 6 or 8 in multiples of $6 to insure full payoffs, the bet should not be made. Also, bets less than $5 on the 4, 5, 9 and 10, and less than $6 on the 6 and 8, will be paid off at only even-money.

To summarize, do not make place bets of 4 or 10, or 5 and 9, for the house edge is too high.

The place bets of 6 and 8 have playable odds of 1.52% and can be used in an aggressive maximize gain strategy, though some players may prefer to stick with the line, come and don't come bets backed by free-odds, the best bets of all.

BIG 6 AND BIG 8

The **Big 6** and **Big 8** are bets that a particular number bet on, the 6 or 8, is thrown before a 7 is rolled. These bets can be made at any time, and are bet by putting the wager into the box marked Big 6 or Big 8.

These bets work just like the place bets of 6 and 8 except that the house only pays even-money on a won bet as opposed to the 7 to 6 payoff you would receive had you made the superior place bet on 6 or 8 instead.

Let's look at the correct odds. There are five ways to throw a winning 6 (or 8, if that is bet), and six ways to throw a losing 7, making the correct odds 6 to 5. The house pays only even-money on a won bet in Nevada, giving them a whopping 9.90% advantage. This makes the Big 6 and Big 8 terrible bets in Nevada, especially when they are compared to the 1.52% odds of the 6 and 8 place bets.

(The Big 6 and Big 8 bets were formerly offered in Atlantic City and were paid off at 7 to 6, like the place bets of 6 and 8. However, the New Jersey gaming commission approved the removal of the Big 6 and Big 8 wager, and they are no longer offered there.)

BUYING THE 4 OR 10

This is an option the casino gives the player when betting on a place number, and though it reduces the odds on the 4 or 10 from 6.67% to 4.76%, the buy bet is still a poor one and should not be made.

But here's how it works.

To *buy* the 4 or 10, you must give the house a 5% commission on your bet. Once you've bought a number, the house will pay off the bet at the correct odds. Thus, your payoff will be 2 to 1, the correct odds, rather than 9 to 5 as is usually the payoff for these place bets.

A 5% commission on $20 would be $1. For any bet smaller than $20, the commission would still be $1 since the craps tables generally carry no smaller units. In these cases, the house edge on your buy bet would be much larger than 4.76%. If you buy the 4 and 10 at $10 each, for a total of $20, the commission would only be 5% of the two bet total, or $1.

Like the place bets, buy bets are not working on the come-out roll, unless you instruct the dealer that the bet is on. They are also similar to the place bets in that they can be increased, reduced or removed at any time prior to the roll. Note that an increased buy bet is subject to the 5% commission on the additional wager.

Some casinos will keep the 5% commission if you decide to remove an established bet or charge an additional 5% if you win your bet and decide to let it ride.

BUYING THE 5, 6, 8, 9

Theoretically, you can buy these numbers as well, but since the commission is 5%, and the house edge on all these place bets is less than that, there is no advantage in buying these numbers.

LAY BETS

The **lay bet** is the opposite of a buy bet, and is used by wrong bettors who are wagering that the 7 will be thrown before the point or points they bet against is rolled. While the bet is paid off at correct odds, it costs the bettor 5% commission on the projected win to get this payoff, and is therefore, a poor bet.

Lay bets, which can be bet at any time, are made by giving the dealer your chips along with the required 5% commission on the projected win. The dealer will place the bet above the point number covered (in the area where the don't come bets are placed) and place a lay button on top to distinguish the lay bet.

To receive the full value on the lay bet of 4 or 10, you would have to wager at least $40 to win $20 (1 to 2 odds). The 5% commission on the projected win of $20 would be $1. Any bet smaller than the $40 lay bet on the 4 or 10 would still be charged the minimum $1 commission (craps tables do not generally deal in currency smaller than $1 chips) making the house edge greater than the 2.44% advantage already built into this wager.

The 5 and 9 lay bets would require a minimum wager of $30 for the player to get the maximum value. The potential $20 win (laying odds at 2 to 3) would be charged $1 commission. Again, a bet smaller than the projected win of $20 would still be charged the minimum $1 commission, and raise the overall house edge on the bet.

The 6 and 8 bets would require a wager of $24 at 5 to 6 odds on a projected win of $20 to get full value from the commission.

HOUSE ALLOWANCE ON LAY BETS	
Points	**House Advantage**
4 or 10	2.44%
5 or 9	3.23%
6 or 8	4.00%

The lay bet can be added to, reduced, or removed altogether at any time.

You are advised not to make lay bets. You'll get much better odds with the wagers discussed in the previous section, "The Most Advantageous Bets."

FIELD BET

The **field bet** is a one roll wager that the next throw of the dice will be a number listed in the field box—the 2, 3, 4, 9, 10, 11, or 12. If one of the numbers not listed is rolled—the 5, 6, 7, or 8—then the bet is lost.

The field bet can be made at any time and is done by placing the wager in the area marked "Field".

At first glance, the bet seems attractive. There are seven winning numbers listed in the field box, and two of these numbers, the 2 and the 12, pay double if they are rolled. In some casinos, the 2 or 12 pays triple. The other winning numbers, the 3, 4, 9, 10, and 11 pay even-money. But let's look closer.

The losing numbers, the 5, 6, 7, and 8, are the most frequently rolled numbers, and make up a total of 20 losing combinations. (Four ways to roll a 5, five ways to roll a 6, fives ways to make an 8, and six ways to roll a 7 = 20). Adding up all the other numbers gives us a total of only 16 winning combinations. The 2 to 1 bonus on the 2 and the 12 is actually worth one more combination each for a total of 18 winning units, and where the 12 (or 2) is paid at 3 to 1, we get a total of 19 winners.

However, there are 20 combinations that will beat us, giving the house an edge of 5.56% when the 2 and 12 are paid at 2 to 1, and 2.78% when one is paid at 2 to 1 and the other at 3 to 1.

In either case, the house advantage is much larger than other bets available at craps. Therefore, I recommend against making field bets.

PROPOSITION, OR CENTER BETS

The **proposition**, or **center bets**, as they are sometimes called, are located at the center of the layout, and are made by either giving the chips to the dealer who will pass them along to the stickman, or, as with the hardways bet or craps-eleven bet, they can sometimes be tossed directly to the stickman.

The central area of the layout is under the complete domain of the stickman, and though he will physically handle the placing and removing of bets in this area, it is with the dealer that you will generally make your bets and receive your payoffs.

The proposition bets are the worst bets you can make at craps and should never be made. The house advantage ranges as high as 16.67% on some of these wagers—that's an enormous edge.

However, these bets are listed and their odds explained so that you will be fully conversant with all the wagers possible at craps.

Keep in mind that when a proposition bet wins, it is customary for the dealer to only push back your winnings, and to let the original bet ride. The dealer will call out as much; "Up again" the dealer might announce. You may ask the dealer to "take the bet down."

Repeating these bets is a way for the house to perpetuate a wager that is terrible for players. Many players let those bets ride again, feeling if they were lucky once, they could be lucky a second time.

Any Seven

This bet, which is that the following roll of the dice will be a 7, is paid off by the house at 4 to 1 (5 for 1), and is among the worst bets you can make.

There are six ways to throw a 7 out of 36 possible combinations, making the odds one in six of throwing a 7 on any one roll, or equivalently, 5 to 1. Since you are paid off at only 4 to 1, the house maintains an exorbitant edge of 16.67% over the player.

Don't even make this bet in your dreams.

Any Craps

This bet, located at the bottom of the center layout and along its sides, is a bet that the following roll will be a craps—a 2, 3, or 12.

There are four ways to roll a winner. The 2 and 12 account for one way each, while there are two ways to roll a three. The other 32 combinations are losers, making the correct odds 8 to 1. The house only pays 7 to 1, giving them a whopping 11.1% advantage.

2 or 12

The 2 or 12 is a bet that the next roll of the dice will come up a 2, or a 12 if you bet that number, and is paid off by the house at 30 to 1.

Of the 36 possible combinations of the dice, there is only one way of rolling a 2 or a 12, making the correct odds 35 to 1 against rolling either number. With only a 30 to 1 payoff, the house enjoys a hefty 13.89% advantage.

Sometimes a casino may only pay off at 30 for 1 (29 to 1), giving them an edge of 16.67%. This makes no difference, for we won't go near that bet in either case.

3 or 11

This is a wager that the following roll will be a 3, or an 11, whichever you place your money on, and the house payoff is 15 to 1. Since there are only 2 ways to roll either number out of a possible 36 combinations, the correct odds are 17 to 1 (34 losers, 2 winners). The house edge is 11.1%. Where the payoff is 15 for 1 (14 to 1), this edge jumps to 16.67%.

Horn Bet

It takes four chips or multiples thereof to makes this bet. The horn bet is a four way bet that the next roll will be a 2, 3, 11, or 12, in effect combining four poor bets together. The house pays off the winning number at the normal payoffs (15 to 1 for the 3 or 11, and 30 to 1 for the 2 or 12), and deducts the other three losing chips from the payoff.

This sucker bet combines four losing wagers for a combined house edge of 12.50% when the payoffs are 30 to 1 on the 2 and 12 and 15 to 1 on the 3 and 11, or 16.67% when the "for" is used instead of the "to," as in 15 *for* 1 and 30 *for* 1. Never make this bet.

Horn High Bet

This is a five chip wager that the next roll of the dice will hit one of the horn numbers—2, 3, 11, or 12. The "extra" fifth chip in the wager is assigned by the player to the number he chooses, in effect, making that part of the horn a two unit wager.

This bet is indicated by handing the dealer five chips, and saying, for example, "horn high 12," or "horn high 3." Winning wagers are paid as in a regular horn wager except the "high horn" wager which will collect double.

Hop Bet

This one roll wager, which does not appear on the layout, is generally made on a combination of the dice not otherwise offered on the one roll bets, such as 2, 3. If the bet is a pair such as 5, 5, you will get the same payoff as the casino gives on the 2 or 12 bet (30 to 1 or 29 to 1). If the bet is a non-pair, such as 4, 5, which has two ways to win (4, 5; 5, 4), the payoff will be the same as on the 3 or 11 bet (15 to 1 or 14 to 1).

To make a hop bet, give your bet to the dealer or stickman, and call out for example "Hop 54", if the 5, 4 is the hop bet you wish to make.

With the more generous payoff, hop bets give the casino an edge of 13.39%, otherwise the edge is 16.67%. In either case, consider the bet a donation to the casino. Never make these bets.

Craps-Eleven

The stickman will constantly exhort you to make this horrendous bet, which is an appeal to bet the Any Craps and 11 bet simultaneously. We don't want to go near either bet by itself let alone together.

Save your money for the show.

Hardways

Whenever the numbers, 4, 6, 8, or 10, are rolled as doubles, the roll is said to be thrown **hardways**. A roll of 22 is said to be **4, the hardway** or **hard 4**, and similarly with 33, 44, and 55, for hard 6, 8, and 10, respectively.

Rolling the 4, 6, 8, and 10 in other combinations is called **easy** such as 6, 4; **10 the easy way**. Betting *hardways* is betting that the particular number you choose comes up hard before it comes up easy or before a 7 is thrown.

Let's look at the odds involved.

HARD 4 AND HARD 10

There is only one way to throw a hard 4 (22) or hard 10 (55), and eight ways to lose—six ways to roll a seven, and two ways to throw a 4 or 10 the easy way (13, 31, 64, and 46).

The correct odds should be 8 to 1 but the house only pays 7 to 1 for an advantage of 11.1%. As with the other center bets, this bet is terrible and shouldn't be made.

HARD 6 AND HARD 8

There are a total of 10 losing combinations—the 6 ways to roll a 7, and 4 ways to roll a 6 or an 8 the easy way. (There are a total of 5 ways to throw the 6 or 8, and subtracting the hardway, it leaves 4 other combinations). There is only 1 way to throw the 6 or 8 the hardway.

The correct odds of the this hardway bet is 10 to 1 but the house only pays 9 to 1, giving them a commanding edge of 9.09%%. Don't make this bet.

BETS PLAY AS THEY LAY

When you hand the dealer your chips to make a center bet, it is important that you watch and make sure that he gets your wager in the proper area, for the casino rule is that bets "play as they lay." Misunderstandings do occur, but it is ultimately your responsibility to make sure your wager is in its desired place.

HOUSE EDGE: THE BETS

BET	PAYOUT	HOUSE EDGE
Pass Line	1 to 1	1.41%
Don't Pass Line	1 to 1	1.40%
Come Bet	1 to 1	1.41%
Don't Come Bet	1 to 1	1.40%
Pass Line (1x odds)	1 to 1	0.85%
Pass Line (2x odds)	1 to 1	0.61%
Don't Pass Line (1x odds)	1 to 1	0.68%
Don't Pass Line (2x odds)	1 to 1	0.46%
Field: 2 or 12 (pays 2x)	2 to 1	5.56%
Field: 2 or 12 (pays 3x)	3 to 1	2.78%
Any 7	5 to 1	16.67%
Any craps (2, 3, or 12)	7 to 1	11.11%
Any 2 or 12	30 to 1	13.89%
Any 3 or 11	15 to 1	11.11%
Any 3 or 11	15 for 1	16.67%
Horn Bet (2, 3, 11, 12)	2/12: 30 to 1	
	3/11: 15 to 1	12.50%
Horn Bet (2, 3, 11, 12)	2/12: 30 for 1	
	3/11: 15 for 1	16.67%
Big 6 or Big 8	1 to 1	9.09%
Hardways 6 or 8	9 to 1	9.09%
Hardways 4 or 10	7 to 1	11.11%
Place 4	9 to 5	6.67%
Place 5	7 to 5	4.00%
Place 6	7 to 6	1.52%
Place 8	7 to 6	1.52%
Place 9	7 to 5	4.00%
Place 10	9 to 5	6.67%
Lay 4 (5% vig)	1 to 2	2.44%
Lay 5 (5% vig)	2 to 3	3.23%
Lay 6 (5% vig)	5 to 6	4.00%
Lay 8(5% vig)	5 to 6	4.00%
Lay 9 (5% vig)	2 to 3	3.23%
Lay 10 (5% vig)	1 to 2	2.44%

5. WINNING STRATEGIES

The underlying principle of all the winning strategies here is to make only the best bets available, those with the lowest odds, for this gives you the best chances of winning. When used as I suggest, the overall house edge will be only 0.8% in a single odds game and 0.6% in a double odds one. You will never make any bet which gives the house an advantage greater than 1.52%, and in fact, the majority of your money will be placed on bets in which the house has no advantage whatsoever!

You'll play aggressively when winning, so that your winning sessions will be big, and when the dice go against you, you'll reduce your bets or even stop betting altogether. This will maximize your profits and minimize your losses, a smart money management technique that can put winnings in your pocket. And you'll follow the guidelines in the money management chapter, so that once you're winning big, you'll leave a big winner.

This winning strategies chapter is divided into two main sections, one for right bettors, and the other for wrong bettors. You are reminded that betting right or wrong are equally valid approaches to winning, with equivalent odds, and that the choosing of either method is merely a matter of personal style.

Within each approach, right and wrong betting, I'll present the best strategies for the single and double odds game, and also the best methods for conservative and aggressive bettors to follow.

The **Basic-Conservative** methods presented are formulated for the cautious bettor, one who wants to get the best odds possible, but not risk substantial sums, while the **Aggressive** methods are more suited for the heavier bettor, one who is willing to risk more to win more.

The two methods, Basic-Conservative and Aggressive, though, are equally powerful. The choice of one or the other depends solely on your bankroll considerations and financial temperament.

A. WINNING STRATEGIES: BETTING WITH THE DICE

In this section we're going to show how the right bettor, using sound principles of play can lower the house edge to the lowest possible figure, 0.8% in a single odds game and 0.6% in a double odds one.

Using my methods, the majority of your wagers will be made on the free-odds bets, wagers that the house not only has no advantage whatsoever, but which if won, will pay you more than you bet!

You'll use only the best bets in our basic strategies—the pass line, come and free-odds wagers, bets which give you the best chances of winning. Built-in to the strategies are methods to turn winning sessions into big winning sessions without any risk of big losses.

BASIC-CONSERVATIVE METHOD: RIGHT BETTORS

Single Odds Strategy

Our standard bet will be in increments of three units so that we can take advantage of the special free-odds allowances should the points be 6 or 8, whereupon we can back our pass line or come bet by five units, for points 5 or 9, where we can bet extra if the original bet is uneven such as $15, where $20 would be permitted as a free-odds wager.

This allows maximum usage of the free-odds bets, wagers the house has no edge on, and brings the overall house advantage down to the barest minimum possible in a single odds game.

These are the three guidelines of our Basic-Conservative strategy:

1. We will make three unit pass line and come bets until we have two points established, and back both those bets with the maximum single odds allowed.

2. Every time a point repeats, whether as a come or pass line point, we will make another three unit pass line or come bet so that we continue to have two points working for us. If a 2, 3, 11, or 12 declares a winner or a loser on the new pass line or come bet, we will follow with another bet until we get that second point established and then take the maximum single odds allowed on that point.

3. If the shooter sevens-out, clearing the board of all bets, we'll begin the progression again with a new pass line bet.

Let's follow a sample shoot to see how the strategy works.

Player Bets: $15 (three $5 units) on the pass line.
The roll is a 9, establishing 9 as the point.

Player Bets: $20 (special allowance) single odds
    $15 come.
The roll is an 11, winner on the come. The winning bet is removed and the player makes another come bet.

Player Bets: $15 come.
The roll is a 6, establishing 6 as the come point.

Player Bets: $25 free-odds on the 6. Since the second point and free-odds bets have been established, no more bets are made.
The roll is a 9, winner on the pass line. The player wins $15 on the line bet and $30 on the odds for a total of $45. Only one point remains now, the come point on 6, so the player makes a pass line bet.

Player Bets: $15 on the pass line.
The roll is a 7, a $15 winner on the pass line, but a loser on the come point. Since the free-odds bets backing the come wages are off on the come-out roll, the player loses only the $15 come bet and is returned the $25 odds bet.

The next bet should be a $15 pass line bet. The 7 cleared the layout of bets, some winning, some losing, and the new roll will be a come-out roll and the start of a new progression. The player won $75 and lost $15 for a total win of $60 in this short shoot.

Again, the Basic-Conservative bettor wants to have two points working for him at all times during a shoot, and will stop making additional bets once the two points are established, and single odds taken on each point.

AGGRESSIVE METHOD:
RIGHT BETTORS

Rather than playing only two points as in the Basic-Conservative method, this strategy immediately attempts to establish three points. Otherwise, all the principles and methods are the same.

We begin by making a pass line bet. After a point is established, we will make a free-odds bet behind the pass line and a three unit come bet. When the come point is established, we will back that point with the maximum single odds allowed, and place yet another come bet backing that too with free-odds.

Once three points are established, we'll stop betting. Every time a point repeats and is paid off, we'll make another bet, so that at all times during a shoot we strive to have three points working for us. If the come point is made, we'll place another come bet. If it's the pass line, then we'll make another pass line bet. Like always, we'll back all our bets with the maximum single odds allowed.

If the shooter sevens-out, we'll start the sequence over again.

With three points covered using this Aggressive method, you can make a lot of money when the shooter starts rolling numbers, especially when you utilize our strategies for maximizing winning sessions.

MAXIMIZING PROFITS:
METHODS FOR RIGHT BETTORS

The way to win big at craps is to play winning streaks aggressively so when points start repeating, our profits will mount quickly. The beauty of these strategies is that, while we give ourselves the opportunity of making huge profits, we never incur the risk of taking a devastating loss, for we'll only increase our bets when winning.

We won't start playing more aggressively until we're ahead by at least 20 units as Basic-Conservative players and 25 units as Aggressive players. For $1 bettors making standard bets of $3, that means $20 and $25 respectively, for $5 bettors making standard bets of $15, that means $100 and $125, while for $25 chip players betting $75 a play, it means $500 and $625 respectively.

Theoretically, we could increase our bet size before this time, but that leaves our bankroll vulnerable to bad runs of luck. The concept is to play aggressively on their money, not ours.

We wait until all our points are established and working before increasing our bets.

Let's say we're betting $15 as our basic three unit bet ($5 units), and have already established the pass line point with single odds on the 8, and two come points with single odds on the 5 and 10. We now have three points working for us, the basic plan for the Aggressive Method, and see that we're already ahead 27 units.

Our strategy now works as follows. Every time a point repeats and we get paid off, instead of reestablishing an additional come or pass line point at the basic three unit bet, we increase that bet by three units to six units, and back the new bet with maximum single odds. Thus, on a six unit bet, points 4 and 10 can be backed by six units, 5 and 9 by six units, and 6 and 8 by ten units.

(If the bet is uneven on points 5 and 9, more than six units can be bet as a free-odds wager, but if the bet is even and can be paid at 3 to 2, the special allowance wouldn't apply.)

Let's say points 8 and 10 have repeated and we have made six unit bets on the new pass and come wagers. The new points thrown are 9 on the come bet and a 10 on the pass line. So as it stands, we have six unit bets on the 9 and 10 (both bets backed by the full odds) and three units on the come point of 5. Should the 10, our pass line point repeat, our new bet would be six units, for our other point, the 5, still has only a three unit bet on it. Do not increase bets to higher levels (in this example, above 6 units) until all the points have been brought up to the same bet size.

If the streak continues and all the basic pass and come bets have been brought up to six unit bets, begin to reestablish won points by making pass and come bets in units of nine, and of course, backing all these bets with the maximum single odds allowed. Increase bets in this fashion for as long as the streak continues.

This steady progressive increase of bets allows us to maximize the profits resulting from a hot roll while protecting us against a sudden seven-out making serious inroads into our winnings.

As an alternate and more aggressive way of increasing won bets, you could increase each won bet by three units regardless of how many units were already placed on the other points. Thus, a bet that repeated twice in a row, could have a nine unit bet on it while the other points were covered by only three units each.

Your bet increases are in units of three so that you can continue to take advantage of the special three unit single odds allowances.

Do NOT begin new progressions (once a shooter sevens-out) at a level higher than three units. This is very important. A bettor that continues to bet in amounts higher than his initial standard three unit wager is susceptible to a short losing streak wiping out his hard earned gains in a matter of a few bad shoots. You will only bet more aggressively during a hot streak, and will not try to anticipate one occurring.

Once you've had your one great shoot you'll never give the casino a chance to get your winnings back. We'll return to our basic three unit bet. If things go poorly, we'll call it quits soon afterwards, a huge winner. If the shooter gets hot again, we'll start increasing our bets and winnings, always ready for the next big kill.

This is smart money management, the key to success for winners.

VERY AGGRESSIVE METHOD FOR MAXIMIZING PROFITS

Adding the Place Bets of 6 and 8

The main advantage of this hard-hitting strategy is that it allows the bettor to cover the most frequently rolled points, the 6 and 8, during every hot shoot, with a chance to make enormous profits should that hot shoot continue. But to do this requires that the bettor risk larger sums of money, and that he gives the house a slightly higher edge of 1.52% on one or two bets during each betting cycle.

For this reason, many right bettors may prefer to stay with the pass and come bets backed by the maximum free-odds to have the best odds possible at all times, and to use either the strategy for increasing individual bets, or the establishing of additional points through pass and come bets as their method for maximizing profits during a hot roll.

To achieve the best results and minimize the risks involved in using this very aggressive betting approach, we'll follow two rules. First, we'll never make place bets of 6 and 8 (or Atlantic City Big 6 and Big 8) until all our desired points have been established through pass and come bets (according to the dictates of our strategies), and will then only place bet the 6 and 8 if these points are not already covered by one of our line or come bets. The place bets of 6 and 8 and Atlantic City Big 6 and Big 8 should never be made in place of our basic line bets (backed by free-odds), for we don't want to replace bets of 0.6 or 0.8% odds with bets giving the house an edge of 1.52%.

Second, we will employ this strategy only when winning. We don't want to risk accumulation of heavy losses if we're already in the hole, but at the same time, we allow ourselves the opportunity to win big without risking a bad loss.

Following these two rules gives us the best of both worlds. We not only get the good odds on our pass and come bets backed by the maximum free-odds, but can also cover the 6 and 8, the heart of all hot shoots, if they are not already covered.

Though more effective when used in conjunction with the Aggressive Strategy (three points covered), place bets could also be made with the Basic-Conservative Strategy according to the same principles. The strategy also works equally well with the single or double odds game. Here's how the strategy works.

Once three points are established and working in a single or double odds game, you should make place bets on the 6 and 8 if those points numbers are not already covered by the pass and come bets.

Example: The come out roll establishes the 6 as the point, and the following two rolls establish the 4 and 5 as come points. The Aggressive Strategy player now has three points covered and backed by the maximum free-odds allowed. Since the 8 is not covered as a point and will be one of the central numbers if the dice get hot, a place bet on 8 should be made.

Every time a 6 or 8 is repeated, you should make an additional place bet to reestablish the point. If another point is made, say the come point of 4, another bet should be wagered, for we always want three pass and come bets working during each shoot. Should the following roll establish a 6 as the come point, the place bet on 6 should be taken down, for we would rather have the point covered with the lower odds of the line and free-odds bet.

Sometimes only three points will be covered using this method, the 6, 8, and one other, while other times, as many as five points will be covered. For instance, if the first three points covered on the pass and come points are 4, 9, and 10, we would make place bets of 6 and 8—during a shoot, we always want to cover these frequently rolled points.

Keep the level of the place bets of 6 and 8 similar to the level used on your other bets and remember to make these bets in multiples of six so that you can get the full 7 to 6 payoff. And during hot rolls, follow our procedures for increasing the standard pass and come bets, remembering to return to the standard bet size once the run is over.

DOUBLE ODDS STRATEGIES

Whenever you have a choice, you should always choose a double odds game over a single odds game for the additional allowance of the free-odds bet drops the overall house edge from 0.8% to 0.6% when using our methods.

The playing strategies we will pursue in the double odds game are identical to the single odds game except that we will bet in units of two instead of units of three as recommended in the single odds game. This allows us to take advantage of the special five unit free-odds allowance when the point is 6 or 8. Basic-Conservative bettors should establish two points with maximum double odds on each, while Aggressive bettors will want to cover three points.

Follow the procedures for the single odds methods substituting only the two unit basic bet for the three unit bets, and making double odds bet instead of single odds.

MAXIMIZING PROFITS: DOUBLE ODDS GAME

Again, our strategy here will follow that of the single odds game except we'll be increasing our bets by two units instead of three. Basic-Conservative bettors will not begin increasing bets until they've accumulated 20 units in profits, and Aggressive bettors will need 25 units.

Remember to take advantage of the special allowances when the point is a 6 or 8. A four unit bet can be backed by 10 units in the double odds game, and a six unit bet by 15.

When eventually the shooter sevens-out, ending our winning streak, we'll start the next progression again at two units, ready to capitalize on another hot roll should one develop.

B. WINNING STRATEGIES: BETTING AGAINST THE DICE

Though the odds of winning are equivalent to the right betting strategies, 0.8% in a single odds game and 0.6% in a double odds game, very few craps players bet against the dice. Many bettors feel uncomfortable about having to lay odds, putting more money on their free-odds bet than they will win should the bet be won, but as stated earlier, the free-odds wagers give the house no edge betting right or wrong.

However, players that bet wrong don't mind giving the odds, for the roll of a 7, their winner, will occur more often than any point number, and they'll have frequent winners. In addition, should a point be repeated, a losing roll for wrong bettors, only one bet will be lost. The other points covered by the wrong bettor are still in play. On the other side of the dice, the right bettors fear the 7, for when it is thrown, all their established points and free-odds bets are lost.

We will apply the same principles of play as right bettors. We'll make only the best bets available to us, those that reduce the house edge to the lowest possible figure—the don't pass, the don't come, and the free-odds bets.

BASIC-CONSERVATIVE METHOD: WRONG BETTORS

Single Odds Strategy

Our standard bet will be in even increments of two units. Bets such as $15 or $25 are difficult to work with when the point is a 5 or 9, and 2 to 3 odds should be laid. Betting in other unit sizes is equally valid, but you'll find it easiest to work in multiples of $10.

These are the guidelines of the Basic-Conservative strategy:

1. We will make two unit don't pass and don't come bets until we have established bets against two points, and back both those bets with maximum free-odds.

2. Should a point repeat, a loser for us, we will make another don't come or don't pass bet, so that we can continue to have bets working against two points. If a 2, 3, 11, or 12, determines a winner or loser on a new don't pass or don't come bet, we will bet another time until we get that second point established, and then we'll play the maximum single odds against that point.

3. Stop establishing don't pass and don't come bets if a second point repeats. This is an important safeguard to protect us against bad losing streaks.

4. If a 7 is thrown, a winner on all our bets, we'll begin the progression again with our two unit don't pass bet.

5. Follow the recommendations in the Maximizing Profits section for advice on how to increase winnings when the dice are going our way.

As cautious bettors, we'll limit ourselves to a coverage of only two points and strictly follow the safeguard recommended in step three.

Player Bets: $20 on don't pass.
The come-out roll is an 8, establishing 8 as the point.

Player Bets: $24 single odds (laying 5 to 6 odds).
   $20 don't come.
The roll is a 3, a $20 winner on the new don't come bet. Another don't come bet is made to get a second point established.

Player Bets: $20 don't come.
The roll is an 8, a $20 loser on the don't pass bet and $24 loser on the free-odds bet. The new don't come bet now has 8 as its come point. Since only one point is covered, another don't pass bet is made. The next roll is a come-out roll. Should the shooter get hot and make an additional point, we'll employ our safeguards and stop making additional bets.

Player Bets: $24 odds on the come point of 8.
   $20 don't pass.
The come-out roll is a 4, establishing 4 as the point.

Player Bets: $40 odds on the don't pass point of 4 (laying 1 to 2).
The roll is a 6, a neutral throw on this shoot.

Player Bets: No more bets. Two points are established, and free-odds have been taken on both bets.

The roll is a 7, winner on both points and free-odds bets, for a total win of $80 on that throw.

The player has won $100 and lost $46 for a win of $54 on this short shoot. The progression starts again with a $20 don't pass bet.

AGGRESSIVE METHOD: WRONG BETTORS

Our Aggressive strategy follows the same guidelines as the Basic-Conservative method except that we will cover three points during a shoot instead of two, and will stop making additional don't pass and don't come bets if three points repeat, instead of two as advised in the Basic-Conservative method. We'll use the same bets—the don't pass, don't come and free-odds bets, and enjoy the same low 0.8% house edge in a single odds game.

We begin by making a don't pass bet, and backing that with the maximum single odds once the point is established. Then, we'll make two successive don't come wagers, or as many as necessary, until two points are established, and will back those bets with maximum single odds as well. Once we have bets established against three points, we'll stop betting.

Should a 2, 3, 11, or 12, be rolled before all the points are established, we'll make another don't come bet until that third point is set. And we'll strictly adhere to our safeguard. If a third point repeats, we'll stop making additional bets during the cycle, and just ride out the unlucky streak. We never want to bet into a losing streak.

When the shooter sevens-out, a winner on all our bets, we'll start our cycle again, establishing three points with the maximum single odds.

MAXIMIZING PROFITS:
METHODS FOR WRONG BETTORS

The safest and most effective way of winning big at craps is to increase bets only during cold runs*, when the dice are going our way. The concept is to parlay winnings into big winnings. We do this by increasing bets only during a winning cycle, when the dice have already won for us, and never after a losing bet. Players and systems that attempt to regain lost money by increasing their bets only court disaster, for this type of desperate betting leaves one vulnerable to huge losses, and that's bad money management.

We won't start playing more aggressively until we're ahead by at least 20 units as a Basic-Conservative player and 25 units as an Aggressive method player.

This gives us the opportunity to make big profits when the dice are with us, while protecting us against ever getting hurt by a bad run. And, as a matter of fact, if the basic wrong betting safeguards and the stop-loss advice in the money management section are adhered to, we'll never take a crippling loss.

But we're always ready to win big.

Unlike the right bettors strategies where bets are increased during a cycle, we will wait until the shooter sevens-out, a winner for us, before we begin to play more aggressively. Once you're ahead the aforementioned amounts, and the previous betting cycle was a winning one, increase the basic bet by two units.

If all our points were covered by two unit basic bets, we'll now cover the points by four unit basic bets, and if after the shooter sevens-out, we have emerged winners again, we'll continue to bet into the winning streak, and up our bet by another two units, to six units. We'll continue to increase

---

* **Cold** runs favor the wrong bettor.

bets by two units as long as the streak continues, all the time backing the bets with the maximum single odds allowed.

If the basic bet was $10 (two units of $5), the next basic bet will be $20, and then $30, and so on.

Anytime a sequence has been a losing one, begin the following shoot at the original two unit basic bet. In the example above, we would begin again at $10. Smart money management dictates that we only increase bets during a winning streak.

All the time during a shoot, we'll follow the safeguards outlined in the strategies. Basic-Conservative method bettors will stop establishing points should two points be repeated, and Aggressive method bettors will hold their bets if a third point repeats.

Let's follow a progression to see how this works. We'll assume the player is betting $10 as a standard bet and had just won a sequence when the shooter sevened-out. The bettor is following the Basic-Conservative method, covering two points. He's now ahead 21 units ($5 units), and ups the basic bet to $20 (four units).

Player Bets: $20 don't pass.
The come-out roll is a 4, establishing 4 as the point.

Player Bets: $40 single odds on the 4 (laying 1 to 2).
$20 don't come.
The roll is an 8, establishing 8 as the come point.

Player Bets: $24 single odds against the 8 (laying 5 to 6), and makes no more don't come or don't pass bets since his two points are already established with maximum single odds.
The next roll is 9, no effect on the established bets.
The next roll is a 7, $40 total winner on the don't come and don't pass bets, and $40 win on the odds bets, for a total win of $80 on this sequence. The player is still doing well,

being ahead a total of 37 units, and ups the basic bet two units more, to $30.

Player Bets: $30 don't pass.
The come-out roll is a 5, establishing 5 as the point.

Player Bets: $45 single odds on the 5 (laying 2 to 3).
$30 don't come.
The roll is a 2, $30 winner on the new don't come bet.

Player Bets: $30 on the don't come, trying to establish that second point.
The roll is a 10, establishing 10 as the come point.

Player Bets: $60 single odds on the 10. Both points are fully established now.
The roll is a 5, $75 loser on that point ($30 don't pass and $45 free-odds).

Player Bets: $30 on the don't pass. If another point repeats, the player will stop establishing points, safeguarding himself against a bad loss.
The roll is a 7, a $30 loser on the new don't pass bet, but a $60 winner on the 10 ($30 don't come, $30 free-odds), for a total of $90 in wins and $105 in losses. Since this progression was a loser, the player starts the following sequence at the basic $10 two unit bet, protecting his current winnings of 34 units ($170).

Players using the Aggressive method and covering three points instead of the two illustrated in the above example, will apply the same principles—increasing bets when winning, and reverting to the original basic bet if a betting cycle is lost.

DOUBLE ODDS STRATEGY: WRONG BETTORS

Whenever possible, the wrong bettor should play a double odds game over a single odds game, for it lowers the overall house edge from 0.8% to 0.6%. And we always want to play with the best odds we can get—the lower the house edge, the greater our chances of winning.

By nature, the double odds strategies are more aggressive than the single odds games, and are more in tune for players whose temperament demands hotter action. For example, if the point is a 4 and $10 is bet on the don't pass, the single odds bettor would wager $20 (laying 1 to 2) as a free odds bet while the double odds bettor covers that same point with a $40 wager (also laying 1 to 2).

The double odds bettor lays more to win more and therefore needs a larger bankroll than his single odds counterpart. Therefore, to play this strategy, the double odds bettor must feel comfortable with the larger bet levels.

Our double odds strategies are identical to the single odds methods, except that we're playing double odds instead of single odds. We'll begin by making a two unit don't pass bet, and backing that bet by double odds once a point is established. If $10 is the line bet, $40 will be the double odds bet if the point is 4 or 10 (laying 1 to 2), $30 if the point is 5 or 9 (laying 2 to 3), and $24 if the point is 6 or 8 (laying 5 to 6).

Basic-Conservative bettors will follow with a don't come bet and lay double odds on both points while Aggressive Strategy bettors will make two more don't come bets backed by the full double odds, or as many don't pass or don't come bets as needed until three points are covered and then backed by free odds bets.

Like the single odds strategies, the Basic-Conservative players attempt to keep two points working at all times while the Aggressive Strategy players strive for three working points*. When points repeat, new don't pass or don't come bets are made to reestablish another, but should a second point repeat for Basic-Conservative players or a third point for Aggressive Strategy players, then we'll curtail all new betting until the shooter sevens-out, a winner on our remaining bets.

We employ this stop-loss as a safeguard to protect against one really bad shoot wiping out our table stakes. However, should the dice start blowing profits in our direction, we're immediately ready to capitalize on the situation.

We start the next come-out roll fresh, with a two unit don't pass wager, always ready for the streak that will mint chips for us.

DOUBLE ODDS STRATEGY: MAXIMIZING GAINS

It is recommended that you increase your wagers cautiously when playing a double odds game. The mushrooming effect of double odds can rapidly increase the outlay of money on the table, so we want to be conservative in our increases. For example, a $10 bettor may want to increase bets by only $5, since each $5 increase could call for an additional double odds bet of $20 if the point were a 4 or 10. You must use your own discretions for bet increases, possibly one unit per winning cycle.

We'll use the same principles outlined in the single odds Basic-Conservative strategy for increasing bets. We'll increase

---

* This new edition recommends playing three points as a wrong bettor as opposed to playing just two for Aggressive Strategy bettors, as the earlier editions suggested. While the chances of winning are the same, playing two points or three, Aggressive Strategy players want aggressive strategies that can go for the gold, and, upon further consideration, with the player getting the best odds possible in a double odds game, we decided to update our double odds strategy for Aggressive Strategy players and recommend playing the three points.

only during a winning streak and not before we're up at least 20 units, and for Aggressive Strategy players, we'll leave ourselves a cushion of 25 units before increasing our wagers.

6. WINNING STRATEGIES: TRIPLE ODDS

TRIPLE ODDS

Triple odds is offered by some casinos as an inducement to attract bettors, and though this option may only be found from time to time, it is a favorable one for you, bringing the overall house edge down below the 0.8% of the single odds and 0.6% of the double odds games if our strategies are followed.

This free odds bet works just like the single and double odds wagers except that the right bettor is allowed to bet triple his pass line or come bet as a free odds wager, and the wrong bettor can bet to win triple his don't pass line or don't come bet, also as a free odds wager. In other words, in a triple odds game, you are allowed to bet even more money than in the single or double odds games on bets that the house has no edge on. And this means you have better odds and therefore a better chance of winning.

You must realize, however, that the triple odds game is inherently more aggressive, for you're wagering more money per betting cycle than in a single or double odds game. You can win more, but you can also lose more. So before entering a triple odds game, you must choose a bet size that is comfortable for your risk tolerance. If $20, for example, is your average pass or don't pass bet in a single odds game, you may want to lower that bet to $10 to accommodate the greater bet sizes which the free odds bets call for in a triple odds game.

Let's take a look at the triple odds strategies, beginning with the strategies for right bettors.

BASIC-CONSERVATIVE STRATEGY: RIGHT BETTORS

Craps games offering triple odds give you even greater opportunities of emerging a winner, for the additional wagers made on the free-odds bets, wagers the casino has no advantage on, drop the overall house edge below the 0.8% of the single odds and 0.6% of the double odds games if our strategies are followed.

To get the best odds, we'll make only the best bets possible as right bettors—the pass line, come and free-odds bets. We'll bet in standard increments of two units on the pass line and come wagers, and once the point is established, we'll back up to the point with the full six units allowable as a triple odds bet.*

The unit size can be any amount desired. If $1 is the unit size, the standard two unit bet will be $2 and the triple odds wager backing that point will be $6 (six units). If $2 is the unit size, our two unit bet will be $4 and the triple odds backing that point will be $12. Similarly, a $5 unit size means a $10 pass line or come bet and a $30 triple odds bet. For bigger players, $10 units translate into $20 standard bets and $60

---

* Players betting in unit increments not divisible by five, such as $1, $2 and $4 bettors, should bet five units as the free odds wager when the point is 6 or 8 so that the full free odds payoff of 6-5 on these points can be enjoyed. On the other points, the 4, 5, 9, and 10, the full six units should be wagered on the triple odds bet. For players betting in the $1, $2, and $4 range, substitute five unit bets as opposed to six units in our examples when the point is 6 or 8.

Players wagering $10 or more on pass line or come bets should make their bets divisible by $5, such as $15, $25, $45 or $100, so that the full 6-5 payoff can be enjoyed when the point is a 6 or an 8.

triple odds; $25 units into $50 bets and $150 triple odds; and $100 units into $200 bets and $600 triple odds.

Here's the guidelines for right bettors playing the Basic-Conservative strategy in a triple odds game:

1. Betting in increments of two units, we will make pass line and come bets until we have established two points, and then back both points with six units, the full free odds bet allowable. (Players betting in increments not divisible by five will make a five unit free odds bet if the point is 6 or 8.)

2. Every time one of our points repeat, we will make another two unit pass line or come bet so that we continue to have two units working for us. If a 2, 3, 11, or 12 declares a winner or loser on the new pass line or come bet, we will follow again with another two unit bet. We will continue making two unit pass line or come bets until we have reestablished the second point. And we'll back that point with the full triple odds.

3. Should the shooter seven-out, clearing the cloth of all our points, we'll start again, and place a new two unit bet on the pass line.

Let's play through a sample shoot in a triple odds game to see how the strategy works. For argument's sake, we'll use $5 chips as our unit bet. Therefore, $10 (two units) is our standard pass line or come bet.

Player Bets: $10 (two $5 units) on the pass line.
The roll is a 7, $10 winner on the pass line. We collect the $10 winnings and start again with a new bet.

Player Bets: $10 on the pass line.
The roll is a 6, establishing 6 as the point.

Player Bets: $30 (six $5 units) triple odds on the 6. $10 on the come.

The roll is a 5, establishing 5 as the come point.

Player Bets: $30 (six $5 units) triple odds on the 5. We now have two points fully covered with odds and make no more bets.

The roll is a 12. It's a loser for any new come bettors trying to establish a point, but since our points are already established, the 12 has no bearing on our bets.

The roll is a 5, a winner on the come bet and the free odds backing that bet. We receive $10 on the come bet (even money payoff) and $45 (3-2 payoff) on the $30 free odds bet. Since we now have only one point covered, we make another bet.

Player Bets: $10 on the come.

The roll is a 10, establishing 10 as our come point.

Player Bets: $30 triple odds on the 10. Two points are established and fully backed by triple odds so we make no further bets at this time.

The roll is a 9, a neutral throw. The only numbers with any bearing for our bets at this time are a 10 and a 6, which are winners, or the 7, which is a loser.

The roll is an 8, another neutral throw.

The roll is a 10, winner on the come and triple odds bet backing the come point. $10 is won on the come bet (even money payoff) and $60 (2-1 payoff) is won on the free odds wager. Since we only have one point working for us, another come bet is made. Had the 6 been thrown, a winner on the pass line, we would instead make a pass line bet since come bets cannot be made on the come out roll. Conversely, a come bet is now made, for we're in the middle of a shoot, but in either case the odds are the same—come bets and pass line bets are equivalent—the only difference between the two is in the sequence of the shoot.

Player Bets: $10 on the come.

The roll is a 7, a $10 winner on the come bet, but a $10 loser on the point (the 6) and $30 loser on the triple odds wager. The 7 cleared the layout of all bets, some winning, some losing. On this shoot, we won $145 and lost only $40 for a total win of $105. The next roll is a come out roll and we mark the start of the new progression with a $10 (two unit) pass line bet.

AGGRESSIVE STRATEGY: RIGHT BETTORS

This aggressive triple odds strategy for right bettors is very powerful and can net huge profits for the player in a short amount of time if the dice are hot. However, the converse can be true as well. A cold run of the dice can eat up chips rapidly. Therefore, this strategy is recommended only for players whose temperament can handle big swings of fortune.

We employ the same strategical thinking as the Basic-Conservative strategy, making only the best bets possible—the pass line, come and free odds bets—and betting in two unit increments. The only difference is that in the Aggressive Strategy in a triple odds game:

1. We make two unit bets on the pass line and come wagers until three points are established and then back those bets with the full triple odds allowed, six units. (Players betting in increments not divisible by five, such as $1, $2, and $4 bettors, should bet five units as the free odds bet when the point is a 6 or an 8.)

2. Whenever a pass line or come bet repeats, we make another pass line or come bet until we again have three points working and back those points with six unit triple odds bets. As points keep repeating, we continue making pass line and come bets backed by six unit free odds wagers until three points are again covered.

3. Once the shooter sevens-out, clearing the table of all bets, we begin the next shoot with a two unit bet on the pass line.

THE GRANDMASTER STRATEGY

This powerhouse strategy not only reduces the house edge to the barest minimum in a triple odds game (and can also be used in a double odds game), but, additionally, provides you with the most powerful strategy ever developed, one that can transform an otherwise good run into a hot streak yielding monster profits. And the beauty of the **Grandmaster** is that while we give ourselves the opportunity of making a virtual killing when the dice are hot, we never risk a devastating loss, for we'll only mobilize this tiger when we're winning, when, so to speak, we're playing with the casino's money.

The **Grandmaster** is recommended only for aggressive players, ones who want to ride a winning tide all the way in. We're betting more with this strategy, meaning we have more money at risk, and you must feel secure about these betting levels before using the **Grandmaster**. But, again, we take the precaution of only playing the **Grandmaster** when winning. Basic-Conservative players should be ahead by at least 30 units and Aggressive Strategy players 35 units before setting the **Grandmaster** wheels in motion.

For example, $10 bettors (two $5 units) playing the Basic-Conservative Strategy should be ahead $150 (30 units) while an Aggressive Strategy player wants a winning edge of $175 (35 units). Basic-Conservative $50 bettors (two $25 units) need to be ahead a minimum of $750 (30 units) and Aggressive Strategy players $875 (35 units) before playing the **Grandmaster**. Similarly, $2 bettors (two $1 units) want winnings of $30 (30 units) as a Basic-Conservative player and $35 (35 units) as an Aggressive Strategy player.

Theoretically, the **Grandmaster** could be played when losing, but that is foolish, for a continued cold streak can turn a losing session into a nightmare. Intelligent money management dictates aggressive betting only when you are ahead.

Here's how the strategy works.

1. We establish our points according to the strategy we're playing—two points as Basic-Conservative players and three points for the Aggressive Strategy players. When the points are backed by the full free odds bets allowable, as outlined in the strategy section, and we see that our winnings exceed 30 units as a Basic-Conservative player and 35 units as an Aggressive Strategy player, we're ready to kick into gear.

2. Every time a point repeats, we'll collect the winnings and reestablish the pass line or come bet with a four unit bet as opposed to our usual two unit wager, and back that bet with the full triple odds allowable: 12 units. As each point repeats, our new pass line and come bets will be established at four units and backed by 12 unit triple odds bets.

3. When all points are covered by four unit bets, we'll replace won points by six unit bets and back those bets by the full triple odds: 18 units. Do not begin increasing bets to the six unit level until all pass line and come points are established at four

units. We want the escalation of bets to be gradual, pushed higher by repeating points and bankrolled by winnings.

4. Due to the explosive nature of triple odds craps, we recommend that the pass line and come bets do not exceed six units. When all points are covered by six unit bets and 18 unit free odds wagers, we'll replace won points at the same six unit level and continue at that bet size until the shoot is finished.

5. When a shooter sevens-out, clearing the layout of all bets, we'll begin again with our standard two unit bet, utilizing the **Grandmaster** only if another hot streak develops and our winnings are at the requisite levels.

One hot shoot with the Grandmaster is all we need for big winnings—winnings we'll never give the casino a chance to recoup. Should a cold streak develop, we're gone, off to a fine dinner and show, with fuel in the wallet. And should the table get hot again, there's nothing like a little sweetener for the pie.

Let's follow one shoot to see how the **Grandmaster** works.

We're betting in $5 units and playing the Aggressive Strategy, covering three points with $10 bets (two $5 units). Let's pick the action up in the middle of the shoot. Three points are already established, the pass line point of 8, backed by triple odds ($30), and the come points of 4 and 5, both backed by triple odds as well ($30 on each).

The roll is a 5, $10 winner on the come bet and $45 winner (3-2 payoff) on the free-odds wager. We're now ahead by over $150 (more than 30 units) and bring into action the **Grandmaster.**

Player Bets: $20 (four units) on the come.

The roll is a 9, establishing 9 as the come point. We again have three points working for us, and make only a free odds bet behind the 9.

Player Bets: $60 (12 units) free odds behind the 9.

The roll is an 8, a $10 winner on the pass line and $36 winner on the free odds bet (6-5 payoff). The **Grandmaster** calls for a four unit bet on the pass line instead of the normal two unit bet toward establishing the third point.

Player Bets: $20 (four units) on the pass line.

The come-out roll is a 10, establishing 10 as the point. Our points now are 4, 9, and 10.

Player Bets: $60 triple odds behind the 10.

The roll is another 10, the point is made again. $20 is won on the pass line and $120 (2-1 payoff on the 10) on the free odds bet.

Player Bets: $20 (four units) on the pass line.

The roll is a 4, establishing 4 as the new point and also a $10 winner on our come point. We had instructed the crew that we wanted the odds bets working on the come-out throw, so we also win $60 on the free odds bet behind the 4. Normally, free odds bets are off on the come-out throw unless the dealer is instructed otherwise. Since the two points working for us, the 4 and the 9, both have four unit bets, we escalate the **Grandmaster** and make a six unit bet on the come.

Player Bets: $60 (12 units) triple odds on the pass line point of 4. $30 (six units) on the come.

The roll is a 10, a winner on our come point of 10 ($20, 1-1 payoff) and the triple odds bet behind it ($120, 2-1 payoff). The roll also establishes 10 as our new come point.

Player Bets: $60 triple odds behind the come point of 10. $30 (six units) on the come.

The roll is a 7, seven-out. We win $30 on the new come bet and suffer a combined loss of 180 on the pass line and come bets of 4 and 9, both backed by triple odds. However, overall on this shoot, the Grandmaster scored big, winning $481 and losing only $180 for a total win of $301.

On the new come-out roll, we begin fresh, opening the betting with the usual two unit bet on the pass line.

BASIC-CONSERVATIVE STRATEGY: WRONG BETTORS

Triple odds is an extra advantage for wrong bettors, players who bet against the dice, for it allows more money to be bet on wagers the house has no advantage on and thereby lowers the overall casino edge below the 0.8% of single odds games and 0.6% of the double odds games.

To maximize our chances of winning, we make only the best bets available—the don't pass, don't come and free odds wagers. These wagers give the casino the lowest edge of any bets available. With the latter bet, the free odds, giving the house no edge whatsoever.

Our bets are sized in two unit increments for ease of playing. Thus, if $5 is our unit size, then $10 will be the standard bet on the don't pass or don't come bets, and, similarly, a $25 unit means a $50 standard bet. $2 bettors would use $1 as the unit size.

Here's the Basic-Conservative strategy for wrong bettors playing in a triple odds game:

1. We'll make two unit don't pass and don't come bets until two points are established and then back

those bets with the maximum triple odds regardless of the point number we're covering.

2. Should one of our points repeat, a loser, we'll make another don't pass bet, and back that bet with the full triple odds. The idea is to have, if possible, two points working for us at all times. If a 2, 3, 11, or 12 determines a winner on a don't pass or don't come bet, we'll follow with another don't pass or don't come bet, whichever is appropriate, until we have established that second point. We'll then back that bet with triple odds.

3. When a seven is thrown during a shoot, a winner on all our points, we begin the progression again with a two unit bet on the don't pass line.

Let's follow a sample shoot to see how the Basic-Conservative strategy for wrong bettors works in a triple odds game. In this example, $10 is defined as our unit bet, and since our standard bet is in two unit increments, we begin with a $20 bet on the don't pass line to get things started.

Player Bets: $20 on the don't pass line.
The roll is a 3, a winner on the don't pass line bet. We collect our $20 in winnings and make another don't pass line bet.

Player Bets: $20 on the don't pass line.
The come-out roll is a 10, establishing 10 as the point.

Player Bets: $120 triple odds on the 10, the don't pass point. $20 on the don't come.

The don't pass bettor must lay odds, put more money on the free odds bet than he will win, for there are more ways to roll a 7, the winning throw for wrong bettors during a shoot, than there are ways to roll any other number. One comfort of betting wrong is that when the 7 is thrown, all the established don't pass line, don't come and free odds bets are won in one fell swoop. On the other hand, right bettors can win only one pass line or come bet (backed by odds) at a time.

The allowable free odds bet for wrong bettors is determined by the ultimate payoff. For example, on the above $20 don't come bet, triple odds would allow us to win $60. Since we have 2 to 1 odds of rolling a 7 before a 10, we must lay $120 to go after the $60.

Let's return to the shoot.

The roll is an 8, establishing 8 as the come point. We now have bets working on the 8 and the 10. We back up the 8 with $72, laying 5 to 6 odds on the allowable win of $60.

Player Bets: $72 triple odds on the don't come point of 8. We make no more bets at this time. We have two points fully covered with triple odds.

The roll is a 2, a neutral throw for our bets.

The roll is a 5, another neutral throw for our bets. We're betting against the 8 and the 10, and only those numbers, which are losers for us, and the 7, which is a winner, are relevant.

The roll is an 8, a loser on the don't come point of 8 ($20) and the triple odds backing it ($72). We make another don't come bet to establish a second point.

Player Bets: $20 (two units) on the don't come.

The roll is a 5, establishing 5 as the come point.

Player Bets: $90 triple odds on the 5 (laying 2 to 3 odds). A triple odds win of $60 is allowed. There are six ways to roll a 7, a winner, and only four ways to roll a 5, a loser, 2 to 3 odds, so we lay $90 to win $60.

The roll is a 7, winner on the don't pass line ($20) and the triple odds bet backing it ($60), and a winner on the don't come point of 5 and the triple odds bet behind it ($20 +

$60). On this shoot, we won $180 and lost just $92 for a total win of $88.

We begin the next progression as we did the last, with a two unit bet on the don't pass line.

AGGRESSIVE STRATEGY: WRONG BETTORS

Playing aggressively as a wrong bettor can be nerve wracking, for a lot of money can be on the felt during a shoot. But when those sevens start rolling, betting against the dice can be pure heaven. Money management dictates caution, for the more money bet, the more at risk. You must always confine your betting limits to a comfortable range, one within your financial and emotional means. The aggressive strategy presented here is powerful, but recommended only for players ready to risk more to win more.

The Aggressive Strategy for wrong bettors in a triple odds game seeks to establish three points during a shoot, as opposed to just two points during a shoot, as in the Basic-Conservative approach. And, of course, the bulk of the money bet is on the free odds wagers, bets in which the house enjoys no advantage.

Following are the guidelines to the Aggressive Strategy for wrong bettors in a triple odds game.

1. Using two units as the standard bet size, we make don't pass line and don't come bets until three points are established, and then back those points with six unit triple odds bets.

2. Should any of our don't pass or don't come points repeat, a loser, we'll make another don't pass or don't come bet, so that, as much as possible, we have three points working for us, waiting for the

seven to harvest in the winnings. If a 2, 3, 11, or 12, determines a winner on a newly placed don't pass or don't come bet, we'll follow with another, until our third point is established, and then we'll back that point with triple odds.

3. Once the shooter sevens-out, a winner on all our established points, we'll collect the winnings, and start the new shoot with a two unit don't pass bet.

MAXIMIZING PROFITS FOR WRONG BETTORS

Wrong bettors are in great psychological position once a point is established, for there are more ways to throw a seven, the winning number, than any other number. Additionally, the throw of a seven is a winner on all established don't pass and don't come bets. At the very worst, wrong bettors can lose only one established point at a time.

On the other side of the coin, right bettors lose all their established points when a seven is thrown and can win only one point at a time.

However, wrong bettors must play with more caution than right bettors, for the nature of betting against the dice requires larger outlays of capital to wager on the free odds bets, especially in a triple odds game. For example, a right bettor with a $20 come bet needs $60 to bet the full triple odds when the come point is 10, while the don't come bettor must lay $120 behind his $20 don't come bet to cover the full triple odds on the same point.

From the right or wrong side of the dice, the odds of winning are exactly the same in the long run, and neither bettor, right or wrong, has an advantage over the other. Betting with or against the dice is merely a matter of style and personal preference.

However, for money management reasons, we caution the wrong bettor to play a more conservative game. Wrong bettors have more money at stake during a shoot, and, therefore, must play a more guarded game even if everything is turning up a winner. We recommend that any increase in bet size be slow and gradual, and that increase be within the bettor's financial parameters.

Playing triple odds as a wrong bettor is a very aggressive game and should satisfy the appetite of most players. But if a more aggressive game is desired, the following guidelines must be strictly observed.

1. Only increase the bet size when winning: Basic-Conservative bettors should be ahead a minimum of 30 units, and Aggressive bettors a minimum of 35 units.

2. Increases in the bet size must be done slowly and gradually, for the escalating effect of laying the odds as a free odds bettor adds up fast.

3. Should two points in a row repeat, losers on the don't pass or don't come bets must stop betting and wait until the shoot is over. It's important to cut losses when the tide turns. Also, once a winner, you want to quit a winner—that's smart money management.

7. WINNING STRATEGIES: 100X ODDS

10X ODDS

The 10x odds games, which are often found in casinos aggressively trying to attract players, especially craps players, give you an excellent game against the casino, but there is a downside: Players who bet over their head can really take a beating with the large amount of action being bet on the ten times bets.

My best advice in this game is for you to look at the ten times odd bet as being your *average bet* when calculating if this game is appropriate for you. For example, if the typical average bet is $10, at a $1 minimum table, you would want to bet only $1 wagers on the line bets since the bulk of the money will be wagered on the free odds at $10 a clip. This way, you bring the odds closer to an even game with the house, and at the same time, you keep the stakes being wagered at a comfortable level.

When playing high multiple odds games, the same winning strategies apply as in the single, double, and triple odds games for both conservative and aggressive players. Bets should be restricted to the pass, don't pass, come, don't come, and of course, the ten times odds bets. Very aggressive players, as we talked about earlier, can add the place bets on the 6 and 8.

These are the only bets that should be made and will give you the best chance possible to be a winner after a session throwing the bones.

Conservative players can play two points, to minimize overall wagers at risk, while aggressive players can go for bigger winnings by playing three points.

100X ODDS

As casinos compete for more player action, games offering as much as one hundred times odds have been promoted in casinos. While these are great games odds-wise, if you are normally a $5 or $10 bettor, then it would be a giant mistake to fully back your bets with $500 or even $1,000 in free odds for the sake of a few tenths of a 1% gain. In fact, it could be outright catastrophic.

If you normally play $100 chips, then a 100x craps game is great: You should bet $1 on the line bets and use your normal black chip for the $100 free odds, taking full advantage of the one hundred times odds allowance—a wager the house has no edge on.

But if you are a smaller chip player, you must stay within your game and take only as much in the odds as makes sense for your bankroll and comfort level.

Remember, just because a casino offers 100x odds, it doesn't mean you need to take them up on that. A craps game that offers 100x odds actually allows *up to* one hundred times odds. You could wager fifty times, ten times, or even three times odds at these games.

8. MONEY MANAGEMENT

The speed with which money can change hands at craps makes intelligent use of one's monetary resources a vital part of the winning formula. Extreme fluctuations are normal in gambling, and the ability to successfully deal with these pendulous swings of fortune often separates the winners from the losers.

To be a winner, you must have emotional control, for the temptation to ride a winning steak too hard in hopes of a big killing or to bet wildly during a losing streak, trying for a quick comeback, are two of the most common factors that destroy a large number of gamblers. Inevitably, the big winning sessions quickly dissipate into small wins or even disastrous losses, while moderately bad losing sessions can turn into a nightmare.

Smart money management also necessitates that you have a bankroll sufficiently large to withstand the normal fluctuations common to craps. Undercapitalization (or overbetting) can leave you vulnerable in two ways. First, a limited money supply can be devastated by a normal downward trend. Second, and quite common, you may feel pressured by a shortage of funds and play less powerfully than smart strategy dictates.

This leads to the cardinal rule in all gambling, and a point that must be thoroughly understood before you ever go near any gaming table.

NEVER GAMBLE WITH MONEY YOU CANNOT AFFORD TO LOSE EITHER FINANCIALLY OR EMOTIONALLY.

The importance of this rule cannot be overemphasized. A player that gambles with needed funds, gambles foolishly, for gambling involves chance, and the short run possibilities of a player taking a loss are real, no matter how good the odds may be.

Gambling should be viewed as a form of entertainment, both monetarily and emotionally. If you cannot afford the possibility of losing your gambling bankroll, either bet at a lower affordable level, or don't play at all. Players that disregard this rule are no longer playing for fun, and are starting to play compulsively. And playing with what is referred to as "scared money" is a certain way for these gamblers to guarantee themselves painful losses.

The emotional level is just as important. Once the playing of the game becomes a cause for anxiety, for whatever reason, and ceases to become a form of entertainment, then it is time to take a breather. You won't play as well because your mind will be preoccupied by the possibility of losing and perhaps more importantly, you will receive no emotional satisfaction from the game.

The goal is not only to win at craps, but to make the experience of playing as pleasurable as possible. This means that you should never gamble if you're emotionally unprepared to risk money, do not feel confident or alert, or any other factor that will adversely affect your playing.

Play again later on, when you feel more alert and confident, and you will have the necessary ingredients of a winner—emotional control. The casinos aren't going anywhere—they'll be there when you're ready to play again.

Money management skills can be categorized as follows:

a. Bankrolling (total bankroll, table bankroll).
b. When to Quit (maximize profits, minimize losses).

Read this section carefully, for these money management skills will not only protect you from ever losing more than you can afford to, but when combined with our powerful playing strategies, will give you the best chances of winning at craps.

BANKROLLING

The amount of money necessary to withstand the normal fluctuations common to craps vary according to the type of strategy you employ (right or wrong betting), the aggressiveness of your approach (Basic-Conservative or Aggressive), and your expected playing time.

We'll discuss the single session bankroll first for the right bettor strategies, for players betting with the dice.

Right Bettors

SINGLE SESSION BANKROLL • RIGHT BETTORS		
Approach (Points Covered)	Units Needed for a Single Cycle	Table Bankroll Needed
Single & Double Odds Game		
Basic-Cons. (2 Points)	14	100
Aggressive (3 points)	21	150
Triple Odds Game		
Basic-Cons. (2 Points)	16	120
Aggressive (3 points)	24	175

BASIC-CONSERVATIVE STRATEGY

In the single odds game, Basic-Conservative bettors will cover two points through pass and come bets and back both points with the maximum single odds allowed. Since the standard line bet will be three units, and the single odds bet backing the pass and come wagers will be between three to five units, we can expect each point to require a total of six to eight units to be fully covered, or about 14 units to fully cover each cycle of two points.

In the double odds game, our standard line bet of two units will be backed with the maximum double odds allowed, or about four to five units for a total of six to seven units per point. Fully covering a cycle of two points will require about 14 units, the same as the single odds game.

In the triple odds game, our standard line bet of two units will be backed with six units, the full triple odds allowed, for a total of eight units per point. Fully covering a cycle of two points requires 16 units.

AGGRESSIVE STRATEGY

Aggressive strategy bettors will need roughly 21 units to fully cover their three points in a single or double odds game.

To play safe, and give himself sufficient funds, the bettor should have enough of a table stake for about seven betting cycles. The **Table Bankroll Needed** columns in the above charts are computed by multiplying the units needed for a single cycle by seven, and then adding a few units as extra padding.

Wrong Bettors

SINGLE SESSION BANKROLL • WRONG BETTORS		
Approach (Points Covered)	Units Needed for a Single Cycle	Table Bankroll Needed
Single Odds		
Basic-Cons. (2 Points)	10	75
Aggressive (3 points)	15	115
Double Odds		
Basic-Cons. (2 Points)	16	125
Aggressive (3 points)	24	175
Triple Odds		
Basic-Cons. (2 Points)	22	160
Aggressive (3 points)	33	225

SINGLE ODDS GAME—WRONG BETTORS

The standard betting size for both Basic-Conservative players and Aggressive Strategy players is two units in our strategies*.

Our free odds wager in the single odds game will vary from just over two units on the 6 or 8 (laying 5 to 6), to three units on the 5 or 9 (laying 2 to 3), to four units on the 4 or 10 (laying 1 to 2) for an average of about three units per single odds bet. In addition to the two unit don't pass or don't come bet, that adds up to five units per point.

Basic-Conservative bettors will need 10 units, two points times five units, for each betting cycle played, while Aggressive Strategy bettors will need 15 units for a round, three points each covered by approximately five betting units.

---

* For players that bet in unit sizes other than two units, they can figure the table stake needed by estimating the number of units needed for one full cycle of play, and multiplying that number by seven.

DOUBLE ODDS GAME—
WRONG BETTORS

The standard betting size for either strategy here is two units, and we'll back each point by about six units, for a total of about eight units needed to fully cover each point in a double odds game. Basic-Conservative bettors playing two points will need 16 units for a betting cycle while Aggressive Strategy players, who cover three points, need about 24 betting units.

In a double odds game, a two unit bet on the 4 or 10 gets backed by eight units, on the 5 and 9 by six units, and on the 6 or 8, by a little under five units, for an average of six units per double odds bet.

TRIPLE ODDS GAME—
WRONG BETTORS

In the triple odds game, a two unit bet on the 6 or 8 gets backed by a little over seven units, the 5 and 9 by nine units, and the 4 or 10 by 12 units, for an average of 11 units bet on each triple odds wager.

Thus, Basic-Conservative bettors need 22 units per betting cycle to cover two points and Aggressive Strategy players need 33 betting units for their respective three points in a playing cycle.

TOTAL BANKROLL

The longer one plans on playing craps, the larger one's bankroll must be to cover the inevitable fluctuations. The following bankroll requirements have been formulated to give you enough capital to survive any reasonable losing streak, and be able to bounce back on top.

TOTAL BANKROLL REQUIREMENTS RIGHT BETTORS			
Approach (Points Covered)	Single Session Stake	One Day Bankroll	Weekend Bankroll
Single and Double Odds Games			
Basic-Cons. (2 pts)	100	300	500
Aggressive (3 pts)	150	450	750
Triple Odds Games			
Basic-Cons. (2 pts)	120	360	600
Aggressive (3 pts)	175	525	875

TOTAL BANKROLL REQUIREMENTS WRONG BETTORS			
Approach (Points Covered)	Single Session Stake	One Day Bankroll	Weekend Bankroll
Single Odds			
Basic-Cons. (2 pts)	75	225	375
Aggressive (3 pts)	115	350	675
Double Odds			
Basic-Cons. (2 pts)	125	375	625
Aggressive (3 pts)	175	525	875
Triple Odds			
Basic-Cons. (2 pts)	160	480	800
Aggressive (3 pts)	225	675	1100

The bankroll needed for a full day's session should be about three times that of a single session, and the weekend's bankroll should be about five times that of a single session. You should never dip into your pockets past these levels for you never want to get beat bad at the tables.

These bankroll levels give you sufficient room to take some losses and still have enough of a bankroll to play confidently and wait for a hot streak to turn the tables on the casino and make you a winner.

This does not mean the player must have all the money out on the table when playing, but that money should be readily available in his pocket in case it's needed.

As you will see later in the minimizing losses section, you should never use all your table stake in any one session. Instead, you should restrict your losses should luck go against you. This way you'll never get hurt by an unlucky session.

If you arrive at the casinos with a definite amount of money to gamble with, and want to figure out how much your unit size bet should be, simply take your gambling stake and divide it by the amount of units you need to have for the particular strategy you want to play.

If you bring $1,000 with you and were to spend a day using the right bettors Basic-Conservative strategy in a single odds game, you would divide $1,000 by 300 units, the number in the Total Bankroll column, for a basic unit bet of roughly $3 ($3,33). Since right bettors wager in units of three in our single odds strategy, the standard pass or come bet would be about $10.

If you were to play the Aggressive Strategy, you would divide $1,000 by 450 units, for a basic unit bet of $2 ($2.22). Three unit bets would come out to the rough equivalent of betting $5 or $6 on the pass line or come bet, $5 being a good choice in the single odds game for we could use the special odds bet allowance when the point is a 6 or an 8.

Similarly, a player who likes to bet against the dice and has brought $1,500 for a single day's gambling would bet in $10 units if playing the Aggressive Strategy in a single odds game. We divide $1,500 by 350 for the rough equivalent of $5 ($4.29), and since our strategies call for bets in increments of two units, the standard don't come or don't pass wager will be $10.

However, we advise against you overdoing it at the craps tables, for though we have reduced the house edge to the lowest possible amount, and given you the best chance of winning, that small house edge can grind out a player over extended sessions of play.

WHEN TO QUIT

What often separates the winners from the losers is that the winners, when winning, leave the table a winner, and when losing, restrict their losses to affordable amounts. Smart gamblers never allow themselves to get destroyed at the table.

As a player, you have one big advantage that, if properly used, will assure you success as a gambler—you can quit playing whenever you want to. To come out ahead, you must minimize your losses when you lose and maximize your gains when you win. This way, your winning session will eclipse your losing sessions and you will come out an overall winner.

Our winning strategies for both the right and wrong bettors, Basic-Conservative or Aggressive style, are carefully formulated to not only give the player the best odds possible to receive at craps, but also to allow this minimize loss, maximize gain principle to work to our advantage.

We will stick by the principle stressed throughout the winning strategies section: When losing, we will reduce our bets or stop betting altogether, and when winning, and only when winning, we will increase our bets to maximize profits during winning streaks.

MINIMIZING LOSSES

Here are some simple guidelines that, if followed, will save you a lot of money. You'll notice that our stop-loss limits are less than the recommended single session table stakes.

1. **Right bettors:** Limit your table losses to 70 units for Basic-Conservative bettors, and 100 units for Aggressive bettors. If betting $5 chips ($15 standard line bet), never lose more than $350 and $500 respectively in any one session; if $1 chips ($3 standard line bet), then $70 for Basic-Conservative bettors and $100 for Aggressive bettors.

    In a triple odds game, limit table losses to 80 units for Basic-Conservative bettors, and 120 units for Aggressive bettors.

    Wrong bettors: Wrong bettors should limit their table losses to the same levels as right bettors in single and double odds games, but in a triple odds game, loss limits should be 110 units for the Basic-Conservative players and 165 units for the Aggressive players.

    Do not dig in for more money, and you can never be a big loser. Take a break, try again later. You never want to get into a position where losing so much in one session totally demoralizes you.

2. Never increase your bet range beyond your bankroll capabilities. In other words, always bet within your means.

3. Never increase your bet size to catch up and break even. Raising it will not change the odds of the game, nor will it change your luck. What it will do is make your chances of taking a terrible beating frighteningly high. Do not get into a position where losing so much in one session destroys any

reasonable chance of coming out even. You can't win all the time. Rest a while, you'll get them later.

PROTECTING WINS

Once winning, the most important thing in craps is to walk away a winner. There is nothing worse than leaving the table a loser after having been up a lot of money. Once your wins at a table have exceeded half to two-thirds your table stake (or less if you desire), you should put aside a substantial portion of those funds into a "don't touch" pile, and play with the rest of the winnings.

If a losing streak ensues and you lose that winning buffer, you have protected yourself. You walk away with winnings in your pocket.

Let's say you're playing the Basic-Conservative strategy and are in the middle of a hot run. You see that you're ahead 80 units. Put away 40 of those units, and play with the other 40. As long as the hot run continues, you will continually put winnings aside into the "don't touch" pile, and of course, according to our maximize gains strategies, we'll increase bets.

However, once that streak ends, and our buffer seems to be wearing away, quit and you'll quit a big winner.

9. FIFTEEN POINTS OF DICE ETIQUETTE

Like all games, craps has its own unique rules of etiquette. You won't look like a pro right out of the gate, but understanding the following fifteen rules of etiquette will make your craps experience as smooth as possible.

1. USE ONLY ONE HAND TO SHAKE THE DICE

The casinos want you to use only one hand when shaking the dice. The reason is simple: It's a precaution against players switching dice, which is harder to do one-handed. It's like blackjack, where players are supposed to handle cards one-handed for the very same reason.

2. DO NOT REMOVE THE DICE FROM VIEW OR OFF THE TABLE

Unless the dice are clasped in a player's hand ready to be thrown, the boxman wants to see those dice at *all* times. Once the dice are brought behind the table or out of view, the possibilities for cheats to exchange crooked dice for the legitimate ones are enhanced. When the dice go out of view, the boxman will likely request that the dice be subject to inspection. He may also require that you choose new dice. Changing the dice slows the game down and could derail the momentum of a hot roll if you're in the middle of a winning streak.

3. MAKE SURE THE DICE BOUNCE OFF THE FAR END OF THE TABLE

The house wants the dice to carom off the far wall to prevent manipulators from "non-randomizing" the rolls. In other words, rolling the dice with a pretty good idea of what will be rolled. If you throw too short too often, the dealers will remove your privileges as a shooter and they could take the extreme step of disallowing the throw if this action becomes flagrant.

4. DO NOT BET AFTER THE SHOOTER HAS THE DICE

All bets are supposed to be placed before the stickman pushes the dice back to the shooter. Late bets cause confusion, and sometimes anger, when wagers are disallowed that otherwise would have won. Late betting makes it difficult for the craps personnel to keep track of late bets, especially when the table is hopping with a lot of action.

5. DON'T THROW YOUR CHIPS

Dealers, and often other players, get annoyed when chips are errantly tossed at the dealers and they have to chase the rolling chips. This can cause havoc when chips land on or collide with other chips, and more than anything else, it slows the game down while the dealers restore chips to their proper positions. The correct way to place center or proposition bets is to place them on the table and announce your wager. The stickman will take over from there and move your wager to its proper spot.

6. DON'T TOUCH YOUR CHIPS WHILE THE SHOOTER IS IN MOTION

Once the shooter begins his dice-throwing motion, you should remove your hands from the table. It is a craps no-no to interfere with the dice, or to adjust, increase, decrease your bets, or otherwise mess with your chips once the shooter is ready to release the bones. You don't want the dice to hit your hand and cause a losing roll for the table. Players that lose bets will blame you for their bad luck causing you to become an object of scorn at a craps table. Shooters and players that are betting "right" want all dice throws to be unobstructed by foreign hands.

7. DON'T CRAMP THE SHOOTER

If you are new to the table or are adjusting your real estate, it is bad form to cramp the shooter as he is getting ready to release. Like all gamblers, craps players are particularly superstitious. Getting in the way of a shooter will be perceived as altering his luck and the table luck. Should an unlucky toss hit the felt, you could be blamed.

8. DON'T UNNECESSARILY SLOW UP THE GAME

Craps is all about momentum and speed for the players. Not that the game is run at a breakneck pace, but players don't want anything to interfere with the regular rhythm of play, including overly long dice-shaking, questions at inopportune times, late betting, or taking too long to decide wagers or pick up winning chips

9. DON'T FOUL THE TABLE

Do not hold your drinks or smokes over the table. Specifically, don't put them *on* the layout. Spilled drinks cause delays and angry players. Craps players want action and dice rolls, not delays because a sloppy drunk or player spilled a drink on the layout causing the game to be stopped. Similarly, ashes sometimes get spread all over the felt and need to be cleaned up before play can be resumed.

10. DO NOT CRITICIZE OTHER PLAYERS' WAGERS

Every player has the right to bet as much as he or she desires. It is the player's money, not yours. Just because a player may be making bets counter to your wagers, or bets that you consider foolish, you do not have the right to put that player down. It is common courtesy to mind your own bets.

11. WHEN BETTING WRONG, BET QUIETLY

Most players bet "right," that is, with the dice, making pass, come and place bets. The wrong bettors, those wagering on don't pass and don't come bets, are typically in the vast minority. Rooting loudly against the majority of bettors at the table is bad form and unpopular. It is okay to bet as you like, but when betting wrong, bet quietly because your wins are losses for most players.

12. DON'T ANNOUNCE THE WORD "SEVEN" IN THE MIDDLE OF A ROLL

Craps players are superstitious. Your fellow players do not look kindly at the dreaded seven, which will kill a roll once a point is established.

13. TIPPING IS CUSTOMARY

As in a restaurant, tipping for good service is expected. It is up to you to decide if you want to tip and how much. The customary tipping method is to make a bet for the dealers alongside one of your own bets. Typically, players make proposition bets for the dealer, but given that these are low percentage bets, you're better off making a line bet instead. This gives both the dealers and you a better chance of winning.

14. NEVER HAND MONEY OR CHIPS TO THE DEALER

As a protection against cheating, physical contact with craps personnel is not allowed. When you want to place bets, color up or down or get chips, place your chips or cash on the table and let the dealer pick up the currency from there.

15. DON'T BE A POOR SPORT

A certain amount of complaining is expected when the dice don't go your way, losses mount up, or a winning streak is stymied. But nobody, in craps or anywhere else in life, wants to be around a constant moaner. Take your losses like a champ to keep the game as fun as it can be, despite the bad mojo.

10. TEN QUESTIONS AND ANSWERS

This chapter extracts ten questions I've received over the years and the answers I've given to readers. Perhaps these questions will be ones that you yourself have. The answers and the reasoning behind them should give you a better understanding of craps.

1. LUCKY WITH PROP BETS, BUT UNLUCKY WITH THE GAME?

QUESTION

My mind says I can't win by making proposition bets, but I can't seem to help myself as I love the prop bets. The fact is that I have some pretty good sessions and pick up some good wins when I get on a roll and start hitting my props. The problem is that I just have bad luck sometimes. If it weren't for that, I'd be a big winner at craps. If I could just knock out one of those bad sessions per ten, I'd have them! What's your advice?

ANSWER

You have a big flaw in your game, what we call a *leak* in gambling circles. When chance is involved, regardless of the odds of the wager, you're going to have good sessions and bad sessions. That's part of gambling. The problem in your game is that the prop bets you're making are giving away too much to the casino. While you're remembering some big wins, you're forgetting the many, many times that those bets just sat out on that felt and died. If you could add up the sum total of all prop bets you've ever made, you'd be surprised at how much money you've lost making them—despite your memory of being ahead with these wagers. It's called selective memory, and many a gambler falls prey to this syndrome. Selective memory is a problem across all gambling games, and in life itself, because it distorts the actual reality of a situation.

Prop bets are terrible wagers. Making them will drain your bankroll to the point where you'll have little chance of beating the game. That's just the reality of prop bets.

You maximize your chances of winning at craps by making the bets that give the house the least possible edge—the line bets, the free odds bets, and for aggressive players, the 6 and 8 place bets. Conversely, you maximize your chances of losing by playing the "house" bets, the garbage in the middle of the table—the proposition or center bets—that are pure sucker plays.

To your issue, it is not the one-in-ten bad sessions that are beating you. You're going to have those bad sessions no matter what. You are getting hurt by the steady drain of your prop bets. You won't have the big hits when your number is rolled, but you won't be getting pinged to death either. Remove that leak from your game and you'll see better results.

2. 3X-4X-5X ODDS

QUESTION

I'm fairly new to craps and I've found a game where the casino offers 3-4-5 times odds. It sounds like an attractive proposition, but I don't understand what it means. I'm asking for help because I'm heading back to the casino and want to take advantage of these odds if they benefit me. What gives?

ANSWER

In a nutshell, yes, the 3x-4x-5x odds are favorable to you. They were set up by the casinos to allow easy payoffs on the odds bets. Here's how they work. Let's say you have a pass line bet and a number is thrown, establishing a point. If the point is 4 or 10, you can take three times odds behind the line; if it is 5 or 9, you can take 4x odds; and if it is a 6 or 8, you can take 5x odds. This way, all the payoffs on winning bets, regardless of the point, will be the same amount. This makes the odds bets very simple to understand and, of course, given the greater amount you are allowed to wager as a free-odds bet, brings the house edge down (to 0.37%) if the casino otherwise would restrict you to 2x odds.

Let's say you're betting $5 as a pass line bet. On the 4 and 10, you can make a $15 odds bet (3x odds); on the 5 and 9, you can bet $20 (4x odds); and on the 6 and 8, you can bet $25 (5x odds) as your odds bets—hence the 3x-4x-5x odds. Notice how all the winning rolls will result in a $30 payoff, regardless of the point hit.

See the Odds Bets Charts chapter for a further illustration of the various bet amounts and payoffs for the points.

3. THE NEVER-LOSE "PROFESSIONAL" CRAPS PLAYER

QUESTION

I want to be a professional craps player mostly because I was inspired by a friend of mine who has since passed. He *always* made money and regularly got comped at the plush Las Vegas and European casinos. The problem is, he took his secrets to the grave with him. I remember much of his advice, but I can't seem to win like he did. I'm wondering if you might know the hidden piece that will tie it all together. His high-rolling casino life was such an inspiration.

ANSWER

If you want to win like your friend described, you can easily do that by immersing yourself in some fantasy life, for example, creating the golden life in your dreams. But for your awake "reality" state, you're going to need a bunch of ice dropped on your lap. In real life, what he described is not the way it is.

I hear from "professional" craps players all the time, offering to share their craps secrets with me for ungodly amounts of money. Or they want to get their secrets published and "change" the game—and their wallets—with the avalanche of sales sure to come. I also hear the same types of stories from people whose friends or relatives are craps players who never lose.

I'm always thinking, "Really?"

I hear plenty about these never-lose players and the private jets, high-roller luxury suites and red carpet treatment. Believe me, I hear about these wizards all the time.

And boy, if you didn't know better, you'd think they live the grandest of lives. What's not to like with that image? But I do know better. And I'm going to educate you now so that the next time you hear about one of these wonders of the world, you'll be able to read between the lines. That high-rolling players are treated like royalty by the casinos is perfectly believable—but don't think the high rollers aren't paying premium rates for that lavish treatment.

Let me set you straight. Here's the real deal.

1. These never-lose players are, in fact, huge losers at the game of craps. If they're getting flown in, they're paying for every dollar of that with their losses—in triplicate at the very least.

2. These never-lose players are also delusional as to their actual wins versus losses. They choose to remember their big wins, conveniently forgetting the many times they got spanked so bad, it hurt

to sit. Bottom line, though, is that their net losses greatly exceed their net wins. In other words, they're *losers*—and if they're getting flown in, big-time losers.

3. One more truth: The casinos can't wait to get these gamblers back at their high-stakes tables, so their first-class privileges are always ready for them.

How do I know this? Because I've heard these stories countless times and I automatically know that when someone "always" wins, they're degenerate gamblers who can't win. Who else would claim that they always win? This group of people are the *gamblers*, as opposed to *players*, who inadvertently help build casinos. Nobody, not even players that enjoy an edge in their chosen game, can win all the time. So once I hear about the guy that *always* wins, I can't help thinking how I'd want a piece of his action.

Now, let me go back to your original point and explain a thing or two about the *hidden* piece of that system—and I don't care what that system is. Craps is a negative expectation game, which means that no matter what you do, given a fair non-biased set of dice, you will lose more than you will win over the long run, on average. The greater the edge against you, the greater the expectation that you will lose. That is in the long run.

In the short run, anything can happen, from small losses and big losses, to small wins and big wins. Playing various systems and strategies is a lot of fun and can lead to profits in a good session or a few good sessions. But you must keep this overriding rule in mind: *Craps is a negative expectation game in the long run.*

Keep it real. Always have money management as your foremost concern before you ever risk a dollar on the table, and you can't get hurt in the game. That's the not-so-hidden secret.

4. WHAT ABOUT MIXING PROPOSITION BETS IN WITH A WINNING STRATEGY?

QUESTION

I see where you advise to make the pass and come bets and back them with double odds or better, but why can't I incorporate some of the other bets into my winning strategy? There are one or two center bets that I'm particularly fond of, especially when they hit and I get back 11 to 1 or more on my money. I should be able to profitably slip a few of those bets in with my basic strategy, shouldn't I?

ANSWER

I hate to burst your bubble, but the exorbitant house edge on bad bets—and the way I see it, any bet that gives the house more than a 1.52% advantage at craps is a bad bet—devastate your chances of winning. Look at it this way: Craps bets are like taxes. Why *voluntarily* pay the government an 11% or 17% tax when you can pay just 1.4%, 0.6%, or even less sometimes.

If that logic strikes a chord with you, than I have to ask you this question: Why make a C-E bet when you can make a double odds bet on the pass or don't pass lines with a wager that is easily more than fifteen times more profitable in the long run?

5. CONFUSING PAYOUTS WITH PERCENTAGES

QUESTION

I meant to write this e-mail sometime ago. I've read craps books by many of the "name" authors out there, but am still confused. I understand that the house has an advantage of 1.4% on the pass line bet, and when backed by the free odds wagers it drops to 0.8% in a single odds game and to 0.6% in a double odds game. On a come-out roll, a roll of 7 or 11 is an automatic winner for the pass line bettors while a roll of 2, 3 or 12 is an automatic loser. Now, a 7 has six combos and an 11 has two combos, for a total of eight combos out of 36 (8/36) or 2/9—about 22%. However, the 2, 3 and 12 have a total of four combos out of 36 (4/36) or 1/9—about 11%. So, if you win 22% of the time and lose 11% of the time on the come-out roll, that leaves a margin of 11%!

Why not play the pass line without the free-odds bets and have a 1/9 or about 11% advantage?

ANSWER

You are overlooking a basic component of the wager: The pass bet does not consist of *just* the come-out roll. The pass bet also comprises the situations where the bet is not settled immediately, but a point is established. When those rolls are taken into account—that is, a point is established (at this point the pass line bettor is a big underdog)—the total bet becomes a 1.4% edge for the house. You can't just look at one part of the roll and determine the odds. It is not a sound approach; you must calculate the probabilities for the *entire* roll.

6. EXPLAINING THE GAME TO FRIENDS

QUESTION

Seriously, craps is the most confusing game of all for new players. I have some gambling buddies that I like to go to Vegas with, but they never like to hang out at the craps tables. They say it's too confusing for them, so they go to the other games where the play is much simpler. They get the idea of the line bets and the points, but immediately get lost when I start talking about field bets, the C-E and other fun bets on the layout. I love craps and wish they would too. How can I get through to them so they can hang with me at the table?

ANSWER

Herein lies your flaw: You're trying to teach bets on the felt that winning players never make. Stick to the explanations of the line bets and free-odds and let your friends concentrate on those bets. Later, they can learn about all the other exotic bets on the layout, but what they should learn is how bad these bets are, not how to play them. As for the teacher, you need to get your game in order first. Just because a bet is offered doesn't mean that you have to accept it. I mean, would you continually take a bet from a stranger where you were such an underdog that you had little chance of ever winning? And do that over and over again, losing good chunks of change each time? If not, then why do that at the craps table?

7. ARE PLACE BETS MORE PROFITABLE THAN ODDS BETS?

QUESTION

In your book, you say repeatedly that taking the "odds" in craps is the best dice bet you can make. Although I agree that the "odds" reflect the actual mathematical probability of the occurrence, it appears to me that the actual money bet can yield more by making an associated place bet. For example:

A $10 Pass Line bet with $20 odds (a total of $30 bet) would yield the following if won:

$$4 \text{ and } 10 = \$50 \ (2 \text{ to } 1)$$
$$5 \text{ and } 9 = \$40 \ (3 \text{ to } 2)$$

However, an equivalent $30 place bet would yield the following if won:

4 and 10 = $54 (9 to 5)

5 and 9 = $42 (7 to 5)

The 6 and 8 $10 pass line bet with an allowed $25 odds (a total of $35) would yield the following if won:

6 and 8 = $40

However, a somewhat equivalent $36 place bet would yield the following if won:

6 and 8 = $42

My point is this: Although you are correct in stating that the best odds in craps are the free odds, you do not make mention that you can make more money with an equivalent place bet than a pass or come bet with the odds. Would you please comment on this. I am probably missing something here since I find your books very informative and practical in your approach to gambling.

ANSWER

Briefly, how much of a percentage the house may have on a bet—be it 0.00% on odds bets, or 1.52% to 6.67% on place bets (making place bets inherently worse for the player)—is completely different from what the *payout* would be. Using your logic above, it would make more sense to play the lottery for a dollar since the payout can be $50 million for that same bet. You are overlooking the difficulty of having the bet translate into a winner and the relationship between the money invested, the chances of winning, and the expected payout—in other words, the house edge.

Stick with the best percentage bets and you'll have the best percentage results.

8. BETTING RIGHT OR WRONG: THAT IS THE QUESTION

QUESTION

I like betting with the dice and have had good success following your advice to play only the best bets offered. I've cut out all the proposition bets and all my impulsive place bets on the numbers. It's amazing how much better I do now. I corral my impulsiveness for more action by making more come bets until I get all the numbers I want. You've convinced me that playing by the percentages is the more profitable way to go. And more fun! However, I'm really taking your advice to heart and see that betting against the dice gives me slightly better percentages. And while I'm a convert to your percentages approach, I just love betting with the dice. Help!

ANSWER

I'm glad to see your results are greatly improved. Despite all the information out there, it still amazes me how many people throw bad bet after bad bet at the craps table. Besides getting the best bets possible in craps and betting within your means, the other important consideration is that you have fun.

Don't worry about converting to a wrong bettor if you like betting with the dice. The few decimal points gained by playing wrong over right are so small as to be inconsequential. If you're betting millions of dollars over tens of thousands of plays, you might consider the consequences of minute percentage points. But even in that case, if you can afford the big bucks, you should still bet with the dice if you're making smart bets. That's what you like and you're not handicapping yourself by throwing money away on "house" bets.

Clearly, you're comfortable as a right bettor. Stick to the good bets, have your fun, and don't worry about losing out on small change.

9. SHOULD I TAKE 100X ODDS
WHEN I FIND THEM?

QUESTION

I have been reading your book and I find it quite interesting. I do not have the bankroll to play the more aggressive strategies that you describe but I would like to try them one day. Question: Regarding your endorsement for taking full advantage of maximizing the free odds wagers, how do players do at a casino that accepts 100x odds?

ANSWER

I get a lot of questions about the 100x games. Sure, the higher the free-odds bets you are allowed, the lower the overall house edge and consequently, the better your chances of winning. However, the main consideration in 100x games is your normal betting limits. Let's say that you're comfortable making $10 line bets and taking double odds on a few points. Of course, this type of betting adds up, but presumably, you've gone to the casinos with a sufficient bankroll for this type of action.

However, 100x on $10 is $1,000 per bet, which is way over your head. But since they allow $1 pass line bets, you decide to put $1 on the pass and $100 behind the line as your 100x free-odds bets. There is a problem here, though—you're wagering more than ten times your comfort zone! And if you're making a larger pass line bet than this $1, those numbers get scarier.

Slow down, partner! You don't want to put yourself in a position where betting over your head destroys your bankroll—all for the sake of getting a small percentage gain. So in general, it is not wise to take full advantage of 100x odds unless that betting falls within your normal bet range. Under no circumstances do you ever want to bet more than you can afford.

10. HOT ROLLS

QUESTION

I'm a big believer in hot rolls and remember a time or two when I really cleaned up because the shooter kept the dice for more than thirty minutes and kept rolling number after number. I know you stick closely to the math end of things, but all experienced gamblers know that there are hot rolls and cold rolls and the savvy ones can take the good rolls to the bank. Do you agree that it is a good idea to try to maximize hot rolls?

ANSWER

Playing into a streak by gradually increasing bets and pushing for the big win is a valid strategy and I have no problem with it.

However, until I can be convinced that the dice have a brain and a memory—and that's really going to take some doing—the idea that anyone can predict what number or set of numbers is going to come next is pure illusion. Of course, it seems that way when you're in the middle of a hot roll, with every point made being one more confirmation of that belief, but the truth is no one knows what will happen next when you're dealing with random events.

If you really could predict those hot streaks or cold streaks, don't you think that, within twenty-four hours of play, you'd own those casinos courtesy of your wins?

You remember the big wins and sometimes the painful losses, but not all the stuff in between. Again, this is what I call selective memory. If you charted all your sessions, you'd find that the numbers would fall as expected. In the short run, some gamblers will win more than their share while some will be on the other side of that pendulum and lose. In the big scheme of things, it's expected. On a smaller level, we end up with "lucky" players and "unlucky" players. But who's to say that their luck won't change the very next time?

Of course, it is very easy for gamblers to get caught up in hot streaks, and trends, and patterns of all sorts. When you hit it big, it makes a lasting impression and all the winning bettors will walk away with a story and a thick wad of cash. Beautiful, that part—but dangerous as well, because it feeds into a common gambler's fallacy. The fact is that it was a hot roll. And you made money. But did you *know* when it would start—or end?

But back to your question: Is it good to play hot rolls—or cold rolls or choppy tables? In short, yes. As long as you keep your wagers to the high-percentage "player" bets and strictly conform to smart money management principles, using systems to take advantage of streaks is a perfectly valid approach— again, as long as you're aware that predicting the next outcome of a random event is beyond human capability.

As for playing streaks, sure, get yourself a powerful strategy and go for it.

11. THE ODDS CHARTS

This chapter presents various charts on dice combinations to help you better understand some of the bets, payoffs, frequency of wins, and percentages in craps. There are charts for dice combinations, come-out rolls, odds of winning and losing on points, and the odds of winning and losing for every possible combination of points when you have multiple points established.

HOUSE EDGE: FREE ODDS BETS
Combined with Line Bets: To One Decimal Place

FREE-ODDS	HOUSE EDGE RIGHT (Pass Line)	HOUSE EDGE WRONG (Don't Pass Line)
None	1.4%	1.4%
1x	0.8%	0.7%
2x	0.6%	0.5%
Full Double Odds	0.6%	0.4%
3x	0.5%	0.3%
3x-4x-5x	0.4%	0.3%
5x	0.3%	0.2%
10x	0.2%	0.1%
20x	0.1%	0.1%
100x	0.0%	0.0%

HOUSE EDGE: FREE ODDS BETS
Combined with Line Bets: To Two Decimal Places

FREE-ODDS	HOUSE EDGE RIGHT (Pass Line)	HOUSE EDGE WRONG (Don't Pass Line)
None	1.41%	1.36%
1x	0.85%	0.68%
2x	0.60%	0.46%
Full Double Odds	0.57%	0.43%
3x	0.47%	0.34%
3x-4x-5x	0.37%	0.27%
5x	0.33%	0.23%
10x	0.18%	0.12%
20x	0.10%	0.07%
100x	0.02%	0.01%

THE ODDS CHARTS

BY THE NUMBERS
Some Craps Slang

	⚀ 1	⚁ 2	⚂ 3	⚃ 4	⚄ 5	⚅ 6
1	Snake Eyes, Bones					
2	Loose Deuce, Little Joe, Little Joe from Kokomo	Hard Four				
3	Easy Four	Fiver	Hard Six			
4	Fiver	Easy Six, Sixie from Dixie	Natural, Big Red	Hard Eight, Square Pair		
5	Easy Six, Sixie from Dixie	Natural, Big Red	Easy Eight, Eighter from Decatur	Nina, Nina from Pasadena	Hard Ten	
6	Natural, Big Red	Easy Eight	Niner	Easy Ten	Yo, Yo-elevn	Boxcars, Midnight

SINGLE ODDS (1X) CHARTS

In their simplest form, the free odds bets are offered at single odds. This means that the equivalent of whatever amount you bet as your line bet can also be bet behind the line as a free-odds bet, with the house getting no edge. Since casinos don't generally pay in less than full dollar increments, the house allows bettors, in certain circumstances, to increase their single odds bets to allow for full payouts. For example, with bets at $5 or $25, casinos will typically allow you to make your odds bet at a 6 to 5 ratio when a 5 or 9 is thrown, and at a 5 to 3 ratio when a 6 or 8 is the point and there is a bet such as $3 or $15 which cannot complete to the whole dollar. These special allowances allow the payoffs to come to an even dollar amount. (See the chart below for examples.)

At a minimum, you should always take single odds on your pass, don't pass, come and don't come bets, as this lowers the house edge on the combined wager to 0.8%, a good amount less than 1.4% when the line bets are made on their own. This is a great bet for you, far better than many of the other offerings in the casino, even worlds better than many of the other bets on the craps table itself—as in up to 16.67% on the any seven bet! In other words, bettors who make any seven wagers will lose, on average, at a rate more than twenty times as much as you will lose if you are making only line bets with single odds! Or looking at it another way, for every $100 an any-seven bettor loses, you will lose only about $5!

THE ODDS CHARTS

			Odds Bet		
Bet	**Point**	**Multiplier**	**Allowed**	**Payoff**	**Win**
	4 or 10	1x	$5	2 to 1	$10
$5	5 or 9	SA	$6	3 to 2	$9
	6 or 8	1x	$5	6 to 5	$6
	4 or 10	1x	$10	2 to 1	$20
$10	5 or 9	1x	$10	3 to 2	$15
	6 or 8	1x	$10	6 to 5	$12
	4 or 10	1x	$15	2 to 1	$30
$15	5 or 9	1x	$15	3 to 2	$25
	6 or 8	SA	$25	6 to 5	$30
	4 or 10	1x	$25	2 to 1	$50
$25	5 or 9	SA	$30	3 to 2	$45
	6 or 8	1x	$25	6 to 5	$30
	4 or 10	1x	$50	2 to 1	$100
$50	5 or 9	1x	$50	3 to 2	$75
	6 or 8	1x	$50	6 to 5	$60
	4 or 10	1x	$100	2 to 1	$200
$100	5 or 9	1x	$100	3 to 2	$150
	6 or 8	1x	$100	6 to 5	$120

SINGLE ODDS CHART
Odds, Payoffs, Win

SA – Special allowance applies.

FULL DOUBLE ODDS (2X) CHARTS

The double odds game is a fairly common offering. Even when greater odds are offered, players will often restrict their bets to the more familiar—and infinitely saner—environs of the double odds game. The house percentage is just 0.6% when a pass line bet is backed by double odds, extremely low by casino standards.

Note that "full double odds"—as opposed to the straight "double odds"—means that you take two times the odds when the points are 4 or 10 and 5 or 9, but 2.5 times the line bet when the point is a 6 or an 8 and the payout amount won't be to the full dollar. For example, when bets can be divisible by 2, such as $2, $10, $50, and $100, but not $15 or $25.

The following chart shows the odds bets allowed and payoffs for a variety of betting amounts.

			DOUBLE ODDS CHART Odds, Payoffs, Win		
Bet	Point	Multiplier	Odds Bet Allowed	Payoff	Win
$2	4 or 10	2x	$4	2 to 1	$8
	5 or 9	2x	$4	3 to 2	$6
	6 or 8	2.5x	$5	6 to 5	$6
$5	4 or 10	2x	$10	2 to 1	$20
	5 or 9	2x	$10	3 to 2	$15
	6 or 8	2x	$10	6 to 5	$12
$10	4 or 10	2x	$20	2 to 1	$40
	5 or 9	2x	$20	3 to 2	$30
	6 or 8	2.5x	$25	6 to 5	$30
$15	4 or 10	2x	$30	2 to 1	$60
	5 or 9	2x	$30	3 to 2	$45
	6 or 8	2x	$30	6 to 5	$36
$25	4 or 10	2x	$50	2 to 1	$100
	5 or 9	2x	$50	3 to 2	$75
	6 or 8	2x	$50	6 to 5	$60
$50	4 or 10	2x	$100	2 to 1	$200
	5 or 9	2x	$100	3 to 2	$150
	6 or 8	2.5x	$125	6 to 5	$150
$100	4 or 10	2x	$200	2 to 1	$400
	5 or 9	2x	$200	3 to 2	$300
	6 or 8	2.5x	$250	6 to 5	$300

THE 3X-4X-5X CHARTS

You can often find craps tables that offer 3x-4x-5x odds. This is valuable because it allows you to get a higher percentage of your chips on bets that the casino has no advantage on. The free-odds bets are the best ones you can make, so you always want to take advantage of these no-house-edge wagers. 3x-4x-5x means that you can bet three times your pass line wager when a 4 or 10 is the point, four times your pass line wager when a 5 or 9 is the point, and five times your pass line wager when a 6 or 8 is the point. The house edge on the 3x-4x-5x free-odds bets is a low 0.37%, which makes the game very attractive for serious players.

The following chart shows the odds amount allowed and payoffs for various betting amounts in a 3x-4x-5x game. Notice that the free-odds win will always be six times the amount of the original pass line bet.

THE ODDS CHARTS

Bet	Point	Multiplier	Odds Bet Allowed	Payoff	Win
3X-4X-5X CHART Odds, Payoffs, Win					
$5	4 or 10	3x	$15	2 to 1	$30
	5 or 9	4x	$20	3 to 2	$30
	6 or 8	5x	$25	6 to 5	$30
$10	4 or 10	3x	$30	2 to 1	$60
	5 or 9	4x	$40	3 to 2	$60
	6 or 8	5x	$50	6 to 5	$60
$15	4 or 10	3x	$45	2 to 1	$90
	5 or 9	4x	$60	3 to 2	$90
	6 or 8	5x	$75	6 to 5	$90
$25	4 or 10	3x	$75	2 to 1	$150
	5 or 9	4x	$100	3 to 2	$150
	6 or 8	5x	$125	6 to 5	$150
$50	4 or 10	3x	$150	2 to 1	$300
	5 or 9	4x	$200	3 to 2	$300
	6 or 8	5x	$250	6 to 5	$300
$100	4 or 10	3x	$300	2 to 1	$600
	5 or 9	4x	$400	3 to 2	$600
	6 or 8	5x	$500	6 to 5	$600

10X ODDS CHARTS

Certain aggressive casinos, anxious to attract craps players, will offer 10x odds in their craps games. The good news is that the house edge on the combined line and 10x free odds bets is a mere 0.2%. That means that for every $100 bet, you can expect to lose just 20¢ on average. *Two dimes*, that's it. That's not much; in fact it is almost negligible. But there is a price to pay: You need to put a lot of money on the line to get these good odds. If you bet over your head, your risk of going broke or getting hurt by a bad run can be significant. For many players, a 10x game is not a wise investment, despite the very attractive odds.

So before you venture into a 10x craps games, be sure it makes sense for you. To be a smart player, money management is *always* the starting point of any discussion.

THE ODDS CHARTS

			10X ODDS CHART Odds, Payoffs, Win		
Bet	Point	Multiplier	Odds Bet Allowed	Payoff	Win
	4 or 10	10x	$50	2 to 1	$100
$5	5 or 9	10x	$50	3 to 2	$75
	6 or 8	10x	$50	6 to 5	$50
	4 or 10	10x	$100	2 to 1	$200
$10	5 or 9	10x	$100	3 to 2	$150
	6 or 8	10x	$100	6 to 5	$120
	4 or 10	10x	$150	2 to 1	$300
$15	5 or 9	10x	$150	3 to 2	$250
	6 or 8	10x	$150	6 to 5	$180
	4 or 10	10x	$250	2 to 1	$500
$25	5 or 9	10x	$250	3 to 2	$375
	6 or 8	10x	$250	6 to 5	$300
	4 or 10	10x	$500	2 to 1	$1000
$50	5 or 9	10x	$500	3 to 2	$750
	6 or 8	10x	$500	6 to 5	$600
	4 or 10	10x	$1000	2 to 1	$2000
$100	5 or 9	10x	$1000	3 to 2	$1500
	6 or 8	10x	$1000	6 to 5	$1200

100X ODDS CHARTS

You will sometimes find 100x craps games. Seriously, the odds just don't get any better than this for house advantage games. How can they? The casino has an edge of just .02%. In terms of the $100 bet example above in the 10x game where you were looking at a theoretical loss of just two dimes, here the amount is miniscule. Try two *pennies*! But the same caveat goes in 100x games as in 10x games, but at a ten-time multiple—buyer beware. This could turn into a very high stakes craps game, one that many bettors cannot afford.

Remember that for most bettors, the house has a huge advantage—compared to players, the house bankroll is unlimited. The house can handle the up and down swings of luck and have a chance to break even and make money. A bettor on a short financial leash can easily be wiped out by typical fluctuations of luck. Practically speaking, you won't find many bettors dipping into the 100x waters. The few that do usually drop plenty of bets on the less juicy player bets, so the house finds a way to get its pound of flesh.

In any case you've been warned: A 100x craps game offers incredible odds, but depending upon your bankroll and the stakes you play, it is potentially a risky game. The math illustrated in the 100x Odds Chart is easy. It is exactly ten times the numbers of the 10x game, but we've presented the information here anyway so that you can see the numbers in black and white—and the size of the full 100x odds bets for each of the relatively smaller line bets that are the base.

THE ODDS CHARTS

Bet	Point	Multiplier	Odds Bet Allowed	Payoff	Win
		100X ODDS CHART			
		Odds, Payoffs, Win			
$5	4 or 10	100x	$500	2 to 1	$1000
	5 or 9	100x	$500	3 to 2	$750
	6 or 8	100x	$500	6 to 5	$500
$10	4 or 10	100x	$1000	2 to 1	$2000
	5 or 9	100x	$1000	3 to 2	$1500
	6 or 8	100x	$1000	6 to 5	$1200
$15	4 or 10	100x	$1500	2 to 1	$3000
	5 or 9	100x	$1500	3 to 2	$2500
	6 or 8	100x	$1500	6 to 5	$1800
$25	4 or 10	100x	$2500	2 to 1	$5000
	5 or 9	100x	$2500	3 to 2	$3750
	6 or 8	100x	$2500	6 to 5	$3000
$50	4 or 10	100x	$5000	2 to 1	$10000
	5 or 9	100x	$5000	3 to 2	$7500
	6 or 8	100x	$5000	6 to 5	$6000
$100	4 or 10	100x	$10000	2 to 1	$20000
	5 or 9	100x	$10000	3 to 2	$15000
	6 or 8	100x	$10000	6 to 5	$12000

DICE COMBINATIONS

ODDS OF ROLLING EACH COMBINATION		
Dice Total	Combinations	Odds of Rolling
2	1+1	2.78%
3	1+2, 2+1	5.56%
4	1+3, 2+2, 3+1	8.33%
5	1+4, 2+3, 3+2, 4+1	11.11%
6	1+5, 2+4, 3+3, 4+2, 5+1	13.89%
7	1+6, 2+5, 3+4, 4+3, 5+2, 6+1	16.67%
8	2+6, 3+5, 4+4, 5+3, 6+2	13.98%
9	3+6, 4+5, 5+4, 6+3	11.11%
10	4+6, 5+5, 6+4	8.33%
11	5+6, 6+5	5.56%
12	6+6	2.78%

There are 36 possible outcomes when two six-sided dice are thrown. Earlier, we looked at the various combinations that can occur. In this chart, we show those combinations, plus the odds of rolling any of those individual throws on one toss of the dice.

THE COME-OUT ROLL

THE COME-OUT ROLL Right Bettors View from the Pass Line			
Outcome	Roll	Result	Odds
Natural	7 or 11	Automatic win	22.23%
Craps	2, 3, 12	Automatic loss	11.11%
Point	4, 5, 6, 8, 9, 10	Point established	66.67%

This chart shows all the possibilities that can occur for right bettors on the very first roll, before a point is established—the come-out roll—and the odds of that outcome.

THE COME-OUT ROLL Wrong Bettors View from the Don't Pass Line			
Outcome	Roll	Result	Odds
Natural	7 or 11	Automatic win	22.23%
Craps	3, 2 or 12	Automatic loss	8.33%
Tie*	2 or 12	Tie	2.77%
Point	4, 5, 6, 8, 9, 10	Point established	66.67%
*The 2 or 12 is barred (depending upon the casino) and a tie			

This chart shows all the possibilities that can occur for wrong bettors on the very first roll, before a point is established—the come-out roll—and the odds of that outcome.

IF POINTS ARE ESTABLISHED

A POINT IS ESTABLISHED			
Right Bettors			
Percentage Outcome on the Next Roll			
Point (Roll)	Odds of Winning	Odds of Losing	Non-Event
4	8.33%	16.67%	75.00%
5	11.11%	16.67%	72.22%
6	13.89%	16.67%	69.44%
8	13.89%	16.67%	69.44%
9	11.11%	16.67%	72.22%
10	8.33%	16.67%	75.00%

Rolling the established point is a winner; rolling a 7 is a loser. All other outcomes are irrelevant once a point has been established. This chart applies to pass and come bets. The "Non-Event" column refers to all rolls that do not decide the outcome of this bet; that is, the roll is not the established point or a 7.

A POINT IS ESTABLISHED			
Wrong Bettors			
Percentage Outcome on the Next Roll			
Point (Roll)	Odds of Winning	Odds of Losing	Non-Event
4	16.67%	8.33%	75.00%
5	16.67%	11.11%	72.22%
6	16.67%	13.89%	69.44%
8	16.67%	13.89%	69.44%
9	16.67%	11.11%	72.22%
10	16.67%	8.33%	75.00%

THE ODDS CHARTS

Rolling a 7 is a winner; rolling the established point is a loser. All other outcomes are irrelevant once a point has been established. This chart applies to don't pass and don't come bets. This chart, not coincidentally, is the exact opposite of the "A Point is Established: Right Bettors" chart. The "Non-Event" column refers to all rolls that do not decide the outcome of this bet; that is, the roll is not the established point or a 7.

MULTIPLE POINTS ESTABLISHED Right Bettors Percentage Outcome on the Next Roll			
Points (Roll)	Odds of Winning	Odds of Losing	Non-Event
TWO POINTS			
4, 5	19.44%	16.67%	63.89%
4, 6	22.22%	16.67%	61.11%
4, 8	22.22%	16.67%	61.11%
4, 9	19.44%	16.67%	63.89%
4, 10	16.67%	16.67%	66.67%
5, 6	25.00%	16.67%	58.33%
5, 8	25.00%	16.67%	58.33%
5, 9	22.22%	16.67%	61.11%
5, 10	19.44%	16.67%	63.89%
6, 8	27.77%	16.67%	55.56%
6, 9	25.00%	16.67%	58.33%
6, 10	22.22%	16.67%	61.11%
8, 9	25.00%	16.67%	58.33%
8, 10	22.22%	16.67%	61.11%
9, 10	19.44%	16.67%	63.89%

(continued next page)

MULTIPLE POINTS ESTABLISHED
Right Bettors
Percentage Outcome on the Next Roll

Points (Roll)	Odds of Winning	Odds of Losing	Non-Event
THREE POINTS			
4, 5, 6	33.33%	16.67%	50.00%
4, 5, 8	33.33%	16.67%	50.00%
4, 5, 9	30.55%	16.67%	52.78%
4, 5, 10	27.77%	16.67%	55.56%
4, 6, 8	36.11%	16.67%	47.22%
4, 6, 9	33.33%	16.67%	50.00%
4, 6, 10	30.55%	16.67%	52.78%
4, 8, 9	33.33%	16.67%	50.00%
4, 8, 10	30.55%	16.67%	52.78%
4, 9, 10	27.77%	16.67%	55.56%
5, 6, 8	38.89%	16.67%	44.44%
5, 6, 9	36.11%	16.67%	47.22%
5, 6, 10	33.33%	16.67%	50.00%
5, 8, 9	36.11%	16.67%	47.22%
5, 8, 10	33.33%	16.67%	50.00%
5, 9, 10	30.55%	16.67%	52.78%
6, 8, 9	38.89%	16.67%	44.44%
6, 8, 10	36.11%	16.67%	47.22%
6, 9, 10	33.33%	16.67%	50.00%
8, 9, 10	33.33%	16.67%	50.00%

(continued next page)

Points (Roll)	Odds of Winning	Odds of Losing	Non-Event
MULTIPLE POINTS ESTABLISHED Right Bettors Percentage Outcome on the Next Roll			
FOUR POINTS			
4, 5, 6, 8	47.22%	16.67%	36.11%
4, 5, 6, 9	44.44%	16.67%	38.89%
4, 5, 6, 10	41.67%	16.67%	41.67%
4, 5, 8, 9	44.44%	16.67%	38.89%
4, 5, 8, 10	41.67%	16.67%	41.67%
4, 5, 9, 10	38.89%	16.67%	44.44%
4, 6, 8, 10	44.44%	16.67%	38.89%
4, 6, 9, 10	41.67%	16.67%	41.67%
4, 8, 9, 10	41.67%	16.67%	41.67%
5, 6, 8, 9	50.00%	16.67%	33.33%
5, 6, 8, 10	47.22%	16.67%	36.11%
5, 6, 9, 10	44.44%	16.67%	38.89%
6, 8, 9, 10	47.22%	16.67%	36.11%
FIVE POINTS			
4, 5, 6, 8, 9	58.33%	16.67%	25.00%
4, 5, 6, 8, 10	55.56%	16.67%	27.77%
4, 5, 6, 9, 10	52.78%	16.67%	30.55%
4, 6, 8, 9, 10	55.56%	16.67%	27.77%
5, 6, 8, 9, 10	58.33%	16.67%	25.00%
SIX POINTS			
4, 5, 6, 8, 9, 10	66.67%	16.67%	16.67%

This chart shows the odds of winning or losing your bet on the very next roll if you have multiple points established. Every possibility is shown in the chart. If you have a 10 and a 4 established, look in the chart for the "4, 10" listing, as all possibilities are expressed going from the smallest die roll to the largest. Similarly, if you have an 8, 5 and a 6 established, look for the "5, 6, 8" listing in the chart.

Rolling the established point is a winner; rolling a 7 is a loser. All other outcomes are irrelevant once a point is established. This chart applies to pass and come bets. The "Non-Event" column refers to all rolls that do not decide the outcome of this bet, that is, the roll is not the established point or a 7. Note that in a few instances, the percentages may add up to 100.1% because of rounding off to the nearest hundredth. For convenience of adding up to an even 100%, we altered the figure of 30.56% to 30.55% (the actual number is 30.5555…%).

MULTIPLE POINTS ESTABLISHED Wrong Bettors Percentage Outcome on the Next Roll			
Points (Roll)	Odds of Winning	Odds of Losing	Non-Event
TWO POINTS			
4, 5	16.67%	19.44%	63.89%
4, 6	16.67%	22.22%	61.11%
4, 8	16.67%	22.22%	61.11%
4, 9	16.67%	19.44%	63.89%
4, 10	16.67%	16.67%	66.67%
5, 6	16.67%	25.00%	58.33%
5, 8	16.67%	25.00%	58.33%
5, 9	16.67%	22.22%	61.11%
5, 10	16.67%	19.44%	63.89%
6, 8	16.67%	27.77%	55.56%
6, 9	16.67%	25.00%	58.33%
6, 10	16.67%	22.22%	61.11%
8, 9	16.67%	25.00%	58.33%
8, 10	16.67%	22.22%	61.11%
9, 10	16.67%	19.44%	63.89%

(continued next page)

Points (Roll)	Odds of Winning	Odds of Losing	Non-Event
MULTIPLE POINTS ESTABLISHED **Wrong Bettors** **Percentage Outcome on the Next Roll**			
THREE POINTS			
4, 5, 6	16.67%	33.33%	50.00%
4, 5, 8	16.67%	33.33%	50.00%
4, 5, 9	16.67%	30.55%	52.78%
4, 5, 10	16.67%	27.77%	55.56%
4, 6, 8	16.67%	36.11%	47.22%
4, 6, 9	16.67%	33.33%	50.00%
4, 6, 10	16.67%	30.55%	52.78%
4, 8, 9	16.67%	33.33%	50.00%
4, 8, 10	16.67%	30.55%	52.78%
4, 9, 10	16.67%	27.77%	55.56%
5, 6, 8	16.67%	38.89%	44.44%
5, 6, 9	16.67%	36.11%	47.22%
5, 6, 10	16.67%	33.33%	50.00%
5, 8, 9	16.67%	36.11%	47.22%
5, 8, 10	16.67%	33.33%	50.00%
5, 9, 10	16.67%	30.55%	52.78%
6, 8, 9	16.67%	38.89%	44.44%
6, 8, 10	16.67%	36.11%	47.22%
6, 9, 10	16.67%	33.33%	50.00%
8, 9, 10	16.67%	33.33%	50.00%

(continued next page)

MULTIPLE POINTS ESTABLISHED
Wrong Bettors
Percentage Outcome on the Next Roll

Points (Roll)	Odds of Winning	Odds of Losing	Non-Event
FOUR POINTS			
4, 5, 6, 8	16.67%	47.22%	36.11%
4, 5, 6, 9	16.67%	44.44%	38.89%
4, 5, 6, 10	16.67%	41.67%	41.67%
4, 5, 8, 9	16.67%	44.44%	38.89%
4, 5, 8, 10	16.67%	41.67%	41.67%
4, 5, 9, 10	16.67%	38.89%	44.44%
4, 6, 8, 10	16.67%	44.44%	38.89%
4, 6, 9, 10	16.67%	41.67%	41.67%
4, 8, 9, 10	16.67%	41.67%	41.67%
5, 6, 8, 9	16.67%	50.00%	33.33%
5, 6, 8, 10	16.67%	47.22%	36.11%
5, 6, 9, 10	16.67%	44.44%	38.89%
6, 8, 9, 10	16.67%	47.22%	36.11%
FIVE POINTS			
4, 5, 6, 8, 9	16.67%	58.33%	25.00%
4, 5, 6, 8, 10	16.67%	55.56%	27.77%
4, 5, 6, 9, 10	16.67%	52.78%	30.55%
4, 6, 8, 9, 10	16.67%	55.56%	27.77%
5, 6, 8, 9, 10	16.67%	58.33%	25.00%
SIX POINTS			
4, 5, 6, 8, 9, 10	16.67%	66.67%	16.67%

This chart shows the odds of winning or losing your bet on the very next roll if you have multiple points established. Every possibility is shown in the chart. Note that if you have a 10 and a 4 established, look in the chart for the "4, 10" listing, as all possibilities are expressed going from the smallest die roll to the largest. Similarly, if you have an 8, 5 and a 6 established, look for the "5, 6, 8" listing in the chart.

Rolling the established point is a loser; rolling a 7 is a winner. All other outcomes are irrelevant once a point is established. This chart applies to don't pass and don't come bets. The "Non-Event" column refers to all rolls that do not decide the outcome of this bet, that is, the roll is not the established point or a 7. Note that in a few instances, the percentages may add up to 100.1% because of rounding to the nearest hundredth. For convenience of adding up to an even 100%, we altered the figure of 30.56% to 30.55% (the actual number was 30.5555...%).

Not coincidentally, this chart is the exact opposite of the "A Point is Established: Right Bettors" chart.

GLOSSARY

Advantage, Casino Advantage
The built-in odds that favor the casino over the player. Also known as *Edge* or *House Edge*.

Any Craps
A bet that the following roll will be a 2, 3, or 12.

Any Seven
A bet that the following roll will be a 7.

Back Line
Refers to the don't pass area.

Bar the 12
A term found in the don't pass and don't come areas which makes the roll of a 12 (in some casinos the 2) a push between the wrong player and the house.

Big 6, and Big 8
A bet that the 6, or the 8, whichever is bet, will be thrown before a 7 is rolled.

Black Chips
$100 chips.

Boxman
Casino executive who supervises the craps table from a seat located between the two standing dealers.

Box Numbers

The boxes numbered, 4, 5, 6, 8, 9, and 10, which are used to mark the point, and to mark place, come, and buy bets.

Buy Bets

A player option to buy a point number, and get paid at the correct odds. However, a 5% commission must be paid to buy the number.

Call Bet

A verbal bet that a wager is working. Disallowed in many casinos by the indication "No Call Bets" on the layout.

Center Bets

See Proposition Bets.

Color Change

The changing of chips to a higher or lower denomination.

Cold Dice

A streak of losing rolls for the right bettors. Good for wrong bettors.

Come Bet

A bet that the dice will win, or pass. Works just like a pass bet except that it can only be made after a point is established.

Come-Out Roll

The roll made before any point has been established.

Coming Out

A term to designate that a new come-out roll is about to happen.

Correct Odds

The mathematical likelihood that a bet will be a winner, expressed in odds.

Crap Out

The roll of a 2, 3, or 12 on a come-out roll, an automatic loser for pass line bettors.

Craps

Term used to denote a 2, 3, or 12. Also the name of the game.

Craps-Eleven

A one roll bet combining the Any Craps and 11.

Cycle

The term designating the establishing of all bets in a betting strategy.

Dealer

The casino employee who works directly with the player and who handles all monetary transactions and bets.

Dice

The two six-sided cubes, numbered one to six, that are used to play craps.

Don't Come Bet

A bet made against the dice. The bet works just like the don't pass except that it can only be made after a point is established.

Don't Pass

A bet made before a point is established, on the come-out roll only, that the dice will lose.

Double Odds Bet

A free-odds bet that allows the player to bet double his line wager as a right bettor, and double the line payoff as a wrong bettor.

Easy, Easy Way

The throw of a 4, 6, 8, or 10 other than as a pair, such as a 1 and a 5, 6, *the easy way.*

Edge, House Edge

See ***Advantage, Casino Advantage.***

Even-Money

The Payoff of one dollar for every dollar bet.

Field Bet

A one-roll bet that the next roll of the dice will be a number in the field box—a 2, 3, 4, 9, 10, 11, or 12.

Floorman

Casino executive who supervises one or more craps tables.

Free-Odds Bets

A bet made in conjunction with the line, come, and don't come bets, that can only be made after the establishment of a point. The free-odds bet is paid off at the correct odds, with the house having no advantage.

Front Line

Refers to the pass line.

Hardway Bet

A sequence bet that the hardway number, the 4, 6, 8, or 10, will come up in doubles before it comes up easy, or before a 7 is thrown.

Hardway

The throw of a 4, 6, 8 or 10 as a pair, such as 3, 3, *6 the hardway*.

Hop Bet

A bet that the next throw of the dice will be a specific number combination usually not found on the layout.

Horn Bet

A one roll bet that the next throw will be a 2, 3, 11, or 12.

Horn High Bet

A five chip wager that the next throw will be a 2, 3, 11, or 12. The high horn bet distinguishes itself from the regular horn bet in that two units are called out for one of the horn numbers, and that number, if rolled, will pay double since there are two units wagered on it.

Hot Roll

An extended succession of winning throws for players betting with the dice. Bad for wrong bettors.

House

A term to denote the casino.

Inside Numbers

The place numbers 5, 6, 8, and 9.

Lay Bet

A wager made by wrong bettors that a 7 will show before the point number.

Layout

The felted surface of the craps table where bets are placed, paid off and collected, and where the dice are thrown.

Line Bet

Refers to a pass or don't pass bet.

Marker

An IOU signed by a player with established credit at a casino.

Marker Buck

Round disk used to mark the point or indicate that no point is established. Also called *Puck*, or *Marker Puck*.

Nickels

$5 chips, usually red in color.

Odds Bet

See *Free-Odds Bet*.

Off

A designation that a bet is not working on a particular roll.

On

A designation that a bet is working on a particular roll.

One Roll Bet

A bet whose outcome is determined on the very next throw of the dice.

Outside Numbers

The place numbers, 4, 5, 9, and 10.

Parlay or Press

The increase of a won bet, usually by doubling it.

Pass, Pass Line

A bet made before a point is established, on the come-out roll only, that the dice will pass, or win.

Payoff, House Payoff

The amount of money the casino pays the player on a winning bet.

Pit Boss

Supervisor of the gaming tables.

Place Bet

A wager that a particular box number, whichever is bet on, the 4, 5, 6, 8, 9, or 10, will be rolled before a 7.

Point, Point Number

The throw of a 4, 5, 6, 8, 9, or 10 on the come-out roll becomes the point number.

Proposition or Center Bets

The bets located in the center of the layout.

Quarters

$25 chips, usually green in color.

Right Bettors

Players betting that the dice will pass. Pass and come bettors.

Roll or Throw

An individual toss of the dice.

Sequence Bet

A bet whose outcome is not necessarily determined on the following roll but may take a succession of rolls to be determined.

Seven-Out

The roll of a 7 after a point has been established, a loser for pass line bettors.

Shoot

A progression of rolls ending on either an immediate decision on the come-out roll, or the sevening-out after a point had been established.

Shooter

The player throwing the dice.

Silver

$1 tokens or dollar chips.

Single Odds

A free-odds bet that allows the player to bet equal the pass or come bet as a right bettor, and equal the payoff on a don't pass or don't come bet.

Standoff

A tie, nobody wins. Also called a *Push*.

Unit

Bet size used as a standard of measurement.

Working

Designation that a bet is "on," that is, in play.

Wrong Bettors

Don't pass and don't come bettors.

BACCARAT MASTER CARD COUNTER
New Winning Strategy!

For the **first time**, GRI releases the **latest winning techniques** for making money at baccarat. This **exciting copyrighted** strategy, played by **big money players** in Monte Carlo and other exclusive locations, is **not available anywhere else.** Based on the same principles that have made insiders and pros **hundreds of thousands of dollars** at blackjack—card counting!

MATHEMATICALLY TESTED
Filled with charts for **easy reference and understanding**. Contains the most thorough mathematical **analysis** of baccarat in print (though explained in terms anyone can understand). You'll see exactly how this strategy works.

SIMPLE TO USE, EASY TO MASTER
You'll learn how to count cards without the mental effort needed for blackjack! No need to memorize numbers—keep the count on the scorepad. Easy-to-use, play the strategy while enjoying the game!

LEARN WHEN TO BET BANKER, PLAYER
No more hunch bets—use the *Baccarat Master Card Counter* to determine **when to bet Player or Banker**. You learn the basic counts (running and true), deck favorability, symmetrical vs. non-symmetrical play, when to increase bets and much **more** in this **winning strategy**.

PLAY SCIENTIFICALLY TO WIN
Drawing and standing advantage, average edge, average gain, total gain, win-loss and % of occurrence are shown for every relevant hand. You won't need to know these numbers or percentages, but we've included them here so you see exactly how the strategy works. You'll be the best player at the table—after just one reading! Baccarat can be beaten. This strategy shows you how!

This copyrighted strategy can only be purchased from Cardoza Publishing

To order send just $50 by check or money order to:
Cardoza Publishing, P.O. Box 98115, Las Vegas, NV 89193

POWERFUL WINNING POKER SIMULATIONS
A MUST FOR SERIOUS PLAYERS WITH A COMPUTER!
IBM compatible CD ROM Win 95, 98, 2000, NT, ME, XP

These incredible full color poker simulations are the best method to improve your game. Computer opponents play like real players. All games let you set the limits and rake and have fully programmable players, stat tracking, and Hand Analyzer for starting hands. MIke Caro, the world's foremost poker theoretician says, "Amazing... a steal for under $500... get it, it's great." Includes free phone support. "Smart Advisor" gives expert advice for every play!

1. TURBO TEXAS HOLD'EM FOR WINDOWS - $59.95. Choose which players, and how many (2-10) you want to play, create loose/tight games, and control check-raising, bluffing, position, sensitivity to pot odds, and more! Also, instant replay, pop-up odds, Professional Advisor keeps track of play statistics. Free bonus: Hold'em Hand Analyzer analyzes all 169 pocket hands in detail and their win rates under any conditions you set. Caro says this "hold'em software is the most powerful ever created." Great product!

2. TURBO SEVEN-CARD STUD FOR WINDOWS - $59.95. Create any conditions of play; choose number of players (2-8), bet amounts, fixed or spread limit, bring-in method, tight/loose conditions, position, reaction to board, number of dead cards, and stack deck to create special conditions. Features instant replay. Terrific stat reporting includes analysis of starting cards, 3-D bar charts, and graphs. Play interactively and run high speed simulation to test strategies. Hand Analyzer analyzes starting hands in detail. Wow!

3. TURBO OMAHA HIGH-LOW SPLIT FOR WINDOWS - $59.95. Specify any playing conditions; betting limits, number of raises, blind structures, button position, aggressiveness/passiveness of opponents, number of players (2-10), types of hands dealt, blinds, position, board reaction, and specify flop, turn, and river cards! Choose opponents and use provided point count or create your own. Statistical reporting, instant replay, pop-up odds high speed simulation to test strategies, amazing Hand Analyzer, and much more!

4. TURBO OMAHA HIGH FOR WINDOWS - $59.95. Same features as above, but tailored for Omaha High only. Caro says program is "an electrifying research tool...it can clearly be worth thousands of dollars to any serious player." A must for Omaha High players.

5. TURBO 7 STUD 8 OR BETTER - $59.95. Brand new with all the features you expect from the Wilson Turbo products: the latest artificial intelligence, instant advice and exact odds, play versus 2-7 opponents, enhanced data charts that can be exported or printed, the ability to fold out of turn and immediately go to the next hand, ability to peek at opponents hand, optional warning mode that warns you if a play disagrees with the advisor, and automatic mode that runs up to 50 tests unattended. Tough computer players vary their styles for a great game.

6. TOURNAMENT TEXAS HOLD'EM - $39.95

Set-up for tournament practice and play, this realistic simulation pits you against celebrity look-alikes. Tons of options let you control tournament size with 10 to 300 entrants, select limits, ante, rake, blind structures, freezeouts, number of rebuys and competition level of opponents. Pop-up status report shows how you're doing vs. the competition. Save tournaments in progress to play again later. Additional feature allows quick folds on finished hands.